Rebuilding Research Writing

T0322897

Our students must become skilled at finding answers and using information to succeed in college, careers, and daily life. Using inquiry, writing, and technology to infuse passion into the classroom research paper motivates students and results in deeper learning. In this practical, research-based book, authors Werner-Burke, Knaus, and DeCamp encourage you to toss the old index cards and jump-start the classroom research paper so that it is more meaningful, manageable, and effective. Explore innovative ways to help students find engaging topics, collect and evaluate information, and write, rethink, and revise to truly impact their audience. The book is filled with tools and student samples to help you implement the ideas in your own classroom.

Special Features:

- Clear connections to the Common Core State Standards
- Ready-to-use classroom handouts for different stages of the research process
- A handy appendix featuring a sample research project timeline and rubric
- Helpful examples of real student work and assessments
- Research-based foundations that guide and inform how the process unfolds and why it works

Nanci Werner-Burke is a former middle and high school teacher. She directs the Endless Mountains Writing Project, an affiliate of the National Writing Project and is a professor at Mansfield University.

Karin Knaus is in her tenth year of teaching English in a rural public high school in Pennsylvania. She is an EMWP teacher consultant (TC) and has co-directed its Invitational Summer Institute.

Amy Helt DeCamp is a former English teacher and department chair at a public high school in rural Pennsylvania. She is a teacher consultant for the Endless Mountains Writing Project.

Other Eye on Education Books Available from Routledge
(www.routledge.com/eyeoneducation)

Writing Behind Every Door
Teaching Common Core Writing in the Content Areas
Heather Wolpert-Gawron

Common Core Reading Lessons
Pairing Literary and Nonfiction Texts to Promote Deeper Understanding
Stacey O'Reilly and Angie Stooksbury

Big Skills for the Common Core
Literacy Strategies for the 6–12 Classroom
Amy Benjamin and Michael Hugelmeyer

Teaching the Common Core Speaking and Listening Standards
Strategies and Digital Tools
Kristen Swanson

The Common Core Grammar Toolkit
Using Mentor Texts to Teach the Language Standards in Grades 3–5
Sean Ruday

Authentic Learning Experiences
A Real-World Approach to Project-Based Learning
Dayna Laur

Vocabulary Strategies That Work
Do This—Not That!
Lori G. Wilfong

Common Core Literacy Lesson Plans: Ready-to-Use Resources, K–5
Common Core Literacy Lesson Plans: Ready-to-Use Resources, 6–8
Common Core Literacy Lesson Plans: Ready-to-Use Resources, 9–12
Edited by Lauren Davis

Helping English Language Learners Meet the Common Core
Assessment and Instructional Strategies, K–12
Paul Boyd-Batstone

Teaching Students to Dig Deeper
The Common Core in Action
Ben Johnson

Rebuilding Research Writing

Strategies for Sparking Informational Inquiry

Nanci Werner-Burke, Karin Knaus, and Amy Helt DeCamp

Routledge
Taylor & Francis Group

NEW YORK AND LONDON

First published 2014
by Routledge
711 Third Avenue, New York, NY 10017

and by Routledge
2 Park Square, Milton Park, Abingdon, Oxon OX14 4RN

Routledge is an imprint of the Taylor & Francis Group, an informa business

Library of Congress Cataloging-in-Publication Data
Werner-Burke, Nanci.
  Rebuilding research writing : strategies for sparking informational inquiry / Nanci Werner-Burke, Karin Knaus, Amy Helt DeCamp.
    pages cm
  Includes bibliographical references.
  1. Report writing—Study and teaching (Secondary)—Handbooks, manuals, etc. 2. Research—Methodology—Study and teaching (Secondary)—Handbooks, manuals, etc. I. Knaus, Karin. II. Helt DeCamp, Amy. III. Title.
  LB1047.3.W47 2014
  808'.0420712—dc23
  2013034343

ISBN: 978-0-415-73465-3 (hbk)
ISBN: 978-0-415-73207-9 (pbk)
ISBN: 978-1-315-81985-3 (ebk)

Typeset in Bembo
by Apex CoVantage, LLC

Printed and bound in the United States of America by Publishers Graphics, LLC on sustainably sourced paper.

Contents

Meet the Authors

Nanci Werner-Burke has been an educator for almost twenty years, though her literacy and technology geekiness span almost twice that amount of time. She taught grades 7–12 in the public schools before completing her English doctorate in Rhetoric and Linguistics at Indiana University of Pennsylvania.

Nanci has taught at Mansfield University of PA for the past twelve years. She prepares future and current teachers to use technology and good teaching to facilitate literacy acquisition and thinking skills. She has directed the Endless Mountains Writing Project, an affiliate of the National Writing Project, for eight years, and has edited six editions of *Voices of the Twin Tiers,* which celebrates juried writing submissions from regional writers, ages K–adult. She has been a contributing author to professional publications in her fields and has presented at state English and Reading annual conferences, as well as at NCTE and IRA. She lives in a cabin, in a wood, with her husband and precocious 7-year-old.

Karin Knaus is in her tenth year of teaching English. Her child-of-an-English-teacher affinity for grammar and editing led her first to a career in public relations, which she left to go back to school for her true calling, teaching.

Karin has her Master's degree in Education from Mansfield University, and teaches varied English courses in a rural public high school in Pennsylvania. She has always had a passion for finding better and more engaging ways to do things and seeks professional development opportunities at every turn. This led her to the Endless Mountains Writing Project, where she learned the untold magic of teaching writing as a teacher consultant and, ultimately, as co-director of the EMWP Invitational Summer Institute.

Her passions in teaching include research, writing, and helping students to find the books and stories that will make them think and then want to immediately pick up another book. She has presented at state and national English conferences, including several presentations at NCTE. She lives in the small town that raised her, enjoying the outdoors and the company of her family and pets.

Amy Helt DeCamp grew up in small towns throughout Pennsylvania. Her British mother's love for the literature of her home country and Amy's love for words led Amy to seek a career teaching English.

Amy graduated from the University of Pittsburgh at Johnstown with a BA in Secondary Education—English. She also studied both English literature and Shakespeare during two summers at the University of Cambridge in England. She worked for seven years as a high school English teacher at a public school in rural PA, teaching every grade except 11th grade, and was head of the English department. Teaching a ten-page, ten-source research paper helped her discover her passion for teaching research and writing. Additionally, she enjoys teaching and performing Shakespeare and traveling to historically significant places.

She is an at-home parent to three girls, twins and a singleton. While at home, Amy is a teacher consultant for the Endless Mountains Writing Project, enabling her to reconnect with her writing roots and also to present at NCTE. She lives with her husband and daughters in Wellsboro, PA.

Introduction
Kindred Spirits

You're a teacher. That makes us kindred spirits. We've collectively known the highs of teaching: students smiling, laughing, engaged in your spectacular lesson; a much-improved assignment from a student you coached on a skill; an email from a graduate who wants your advice about a good book to read. Of course, we've also collectively known the lows: reading next year's schedule and seeing the dreaded, life-draining lunch duty; bearing the disappointment of a lesson you planned and thought would awe that, actually, sucked all joy out of classroom life for your kids; and then there's the day you announce a research assignment. Remember that scene in the movie *Airplane!* when the passengers find out they no longer have a pilot? The whole cabin descends into chaos, with people trampling others, attempting to escape, and screaming wildly in terror. Often, that kind of image pops into your head when you enter the classroom prepared to make the research paper announcement. *Will that kind of chaos ensue today?* The research paper just doesn't sit well with most kids . . . and consequently, most teachers.

The idea to write this book came to us long after we recognized that the three of us were very different people, at very different places in our lives, who were drawn together by our love of teaching, of language, and of students. As we organized the chapters and worked with the students, we have continued to learn about ourselves and build on our teaching. We have had an incredibly fun time doing it. In the often stressful and always-changing world of teaching, the kids and fellowship of colleagues are what keep us going.

At the start, we wondered what could be possible if we reimagined the traditional classroom research paper from the ground up. In the following pages, you will find new approaches that breathe life into researching, connect best practices with real kids, and aim squarely at moving academic skills beyond exercises and into everyday use.

To really get the flavor of our task, here's a bit about who we are and how/where we dived into this project. Karin is a high school teacher in rural Pennsylvania with a hard karaoke habit. She teaches in a small school with nice kids and terrific teachers, and in a small community, the outlying areas of which reside in one of the dark, no-service areas on the cell phone coverage map. Her kids, like your kids, have access to and training in technology in their curriculum and have been exposed to language arts classes, including literature, composition, and research, even though some will swear that they have not heard of such things.

It is said that children's first teachers are their parents. In this sense, Amy has been a teacher full-time for fourteen years. Seven of them were teaching public high school and seven have been spent at home, as she switched gears to focus on getting her three daughters solidly started in life. As her youngest geared up for her first year with a full school day, she began thinking about how to best prepare for a return to the classroom.

Nanci taught middle and high school before moving on to live in a cabin, in a wood, and work in higher education and teacher development. She is an affirmed tech geek and tries to keep that in check when dealing with the non-believers, and is sometimes successful in that effort.

All three of us are part of the Endless Mountains Writing Project (EMWP) at Mansfield University of Pennsylvania. A site of the federally funded National Writing Project, the EMWP has brought us, and countless other professionals, together as writers and teachers of writing. The EMWP has taken us down many roads, and among the three of us, we have taken on quite a variety of roles in our related professional development presentations and workshops: Literacy Network chef, swashbuckling pirate of style, and that caped literacy avenger Wonder Writer, for example.

In preparation for writing this text, our work with the EMWP took us to Karin's school district and her classroom. We began working with several of her senior high English classes in the spring of 2012, and concluded with this project just before summer 2013. We've made a lot of adjustments along the way, but kept our aim true—revamping the research paper from square one.

Our thanks go out to all of the people in our lives, both personal and professional, who have given us energy and ideas along the way. Shout outs, in particular, to the National Writing Project, and all of our EMWP colleagues. Also, to Angie Martinez, graduate-assistant extraordinaire, certified math teacher, future librarian, and gifted and creative individual. To Matt Getz and Levi Tinney, who gained field experience and contributed to Karin's classroom with lessons on creating citations and dynamic opening sentences, we offer our thanks.

As we wrote (and rewrote!), we tried to keep our work applicable to as many teaching situations as possible, and for teachers with different years of experience. We recognize that you will have a group of different students, in a different context, and we would love to hear about any adaptive suggestions or questions you might have about any piece of this text. Our email addresses are available on the publisher's website so that you can contact any of us.

We also wrote with an eye toward providing a big picture view of how and why to try our methods, with specific examples to illustrate what we (and the students) did. Our goal was to provide a text that will still be relevant and useful to you both now and also down the line. Though resources and tools will change, the need for sound, original thinking and communication will always be in demand, as will the teacher who can develop these skills in their students and keep them moving purposefully forward.

Read, think, question, search and find . . . recognize yourself, a colleague, a student . . . and chuckle, snort, nod . . . enjoy!

All That Rises

Convergence Drives Change

Wax poetic. Bring on the drama. When life gives you lemons, respond with Great Literature! Cosa Nostra Grammatica. Don't Let the Errorists Win! There are a lot of different aspects to being an English Language Arts teacher. Some of them are available on t-shirts. You know, the clever, witty ... nerdy ... kind. You became an ELA teacher because of a love of poetry, drama, literature, grammar, red pens, or a combination of these. For many of us, the research paper represents a challenge that seems separate from these "art" parts of our field. A lot of our students feel this way, too, seeing a great chasm between the task of producing a research paper and anything remotely related to their lives, plans, and passions. We can do *so well* with helping our students explore their identities and the human condition through literature, but as it has traditionally been taught, the research paper is sometimes more an exercise in tediousness than it is in student learning and growth.

Life, Love, and the Literature

You know that there are two parts (at least!) to being a teacher: knowing and loving your content, and then also being able to cultivate this love of language arts and build related skills with your students. People who don't embrace both of those areas will wash out of the profession (or should—life is too short to work every day at something you don't get any satisfaction from, and kids deserve better than mediocrity). It used to be that we "taught the research paper" so that the college-bound in our classes would be prepared for post-secondary academic work. That's changed. Knowing how to find information and be able to work with it is more than just an exercise for academia. It's a skill for survival.

In the modern world, we are constantly surrounded by a flood of information (Bean, Moore, Birdyshaw, & Rycik, 1999). The need and expectation to be information savvy are increasing in the work place and in everyday life. Being able to find information and make sense of it is no longer a skill for the few. Information literacy is a crucial skill for this century (American Association of School Librarians, 2007) and, like writing, is a fundamental need for the many (College Board, 2004). The two skills must be recognized and taught in conjunction if we are to prepare our students for active, modern citizenship and living.

At the core, the research paper is about equipping kids with the tools they need to purposefully explore the world as a means of expanding their own. It's about helping them look for, find, and connect to something strongly, so strongly that they are compelled to put in the effort to read and think deeply about it. They need something that compels them to put in the time to finesse their findings into a work that other people will also want to read, view, listen to, and forge connections with.

It's a tall order. With this book, our goal is to give YOU more of the tools you need to spark your students, build on their skills and interests, and support them at every step with motivating and innovative ideas. Sometimes, the tools we suggest are questioning strategies that are intended to kick-start and extend. Sometimes, they are larger mini-lessons and activities that focus on content and specific skills. Sometimes, they are digital tools that support the processes of searching, dialoguing, organizing, and presenting. Always, they are supported with explanations from the research that is the memory and collective voice of our profession.

This is not a book of blackline masters. There are models and links to many of our resources online, and you can access them at our publisher's website: www.routledge.com/eyeoneducation

We hope that you find them to be useful templates for what you want to try in your own classroom. But there's more to teaching than handing out worksheets, and we all know that, even when some of the "4Ps" (press, parents, publishers, politicians) say otherwise. This book is also not just a list of gadgets and services. Our tools are not meant to be used as cookie cutters.

Technology is a fact of life, and it can enhance teaching and learning significantly, but only when there is a real reason for choosing and using it. Our goal is to offer substance that you can really run with. This text will outline a modern paradigm, one that is needed, one whose time has come, because, as Karl Frisch and Scott McLeod have noted, "shift happens" (Frisch & McLeod, 2007, 2008, 2009, and 2011 . . . as well as by countless other authors and remixers!).

Making changes can be hard. (How long has the U.S. been adopting the metric system?) Maybe there are so many things already working well in your classroom that you don't want to tinker with them too much. Or maybe you are looking for new ways to keep things fresh. Either way, the times they are a-changin', and we'd like to see you be the most prepared you can be to change ahead of the game. The rules and means are changing around your classroom, changing around you, changing around your students. What they will need to know and what they will need to be able to do is on a collision course with their date of graduation, at a rate that is unprecedented in human history. *Everything* you will need to know to get them ready is beyond the scope of this book, but we'd like to contribute to getting you further along.

At least three elements are converging that are driving the need for change:

1. How the education system is structured
2. How we use information to manage our lives, stay informed, and contribute at work and in society
3. How we use technology to boost our interaction with information and with each other

We'll unpack each of these elements and discuss how they are interwoven, then outline how the following chapters fit into this framework. By the time you finish the last chapter you may need to lie down for a while.

(Re)Structuring Education: A History Lesson

Do your students ever really get to or past the war in Vietnam in their high school history classes? Often, the answer is no. One result is that most kids don't see historical events as having shaped the world as it is today, because they "never get to" the past fifty years or so. As this book was being written, the bombing incidents at the Boston Marathon occurred, yet in many adolescent classrooms, even those in the social studies area, this event was not acknowledged or discussed. Do we really need to see something in a textbook or official curriculum before we recognize that it has merit? That seems blatantly foolish, and yet, admittedly, there can be quite a disconnect between the usual curriculum and the world in which our students live and breathe.

To head off a similar oversight here at the start of our discussion about education, let's take a super-quick historical trip through the past 250 years of government involvement in education, and then look more closely at the changes that means for the state of education right now.

Cue up the theme from Jeopardy, and your best inner Alex Trebek voice, and tackle the following:

In what year did the following first occur?

_____ A U.S. federal agency issued a call for federal funds to:
"(1) raise the educational level of the most disadvantaged members of society, (2) promote economic (or "manpower") development through the expansion

of access to learning, and (3) assimilate new citizens into American society for purposes of productive labor"

_____ federally subsidized food and milk purchases were made for school lunch programs

_____ a group of governors, working as part of a think tank, issued a call for academic standards that was felt across the states

If you are not sure of the years, try just putting them in chronological order. If you are in ELA, you are likely able read upside down with little effort, so we put the answers on the next page, in Figure 1.1, Jeopardy Answers. Try your best, check your answers, and then, unlike that kid who has had your hall pass for fifteen minutes, remember to come back here.

How'd you do?

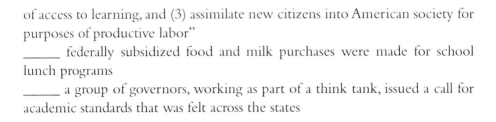

In the Beginning

Large-scale change always has roots in multiple, smaller changes. When No Child Left Behind (NCLB) was unfolding and schools were in the initial rush to respond to the demands of Adequate Yearly Progress (AYP), I often would hear teachers complaining about the program. Some of these complaints were quite justifiable. Others had no roots except for a grumbling resistance to any change. To these teachers, I would often pose the question, "Why are you surprised about this mandate?" After all, it didn't come out of the blue . . .

A quick review of history (as accomplished in by your Jeopardy junket) reveals that the federal government has always played a role in U.S. public education, although that role has been the subject of controversy and has definitely increased *exponentially* in the past fifty years. Federal resources have been a part of American schools since their beginning. With greater allocation of resources come stronger guidelines on how they are to be used.

In recent times, there have been loud, large-scale calls for national educational reform, some from reputable professional organizations and research groups (The National Commission on Writing and the National Writing Project, for example). There have been quieter surges in new and experimental education frameworks and approaches, at the state, district, or classroom level (as in this book!). Add to these the scratched heads of parents and students puzzling over the disconnect (which often results in acting out and sometimes results in dropping out) between the dynamic real world and that of the sometimes-fossilized school system, and you have a snapshot of what

The events are already in chronological order, according to *Federal Education Policy and the States, 1945–2009: A Brief Synopsis. States' Impact on Federal Education Policy Project*, which, despite its title, chronicles back to 1785, when the federal government's role in education focused mainly on land grants for post-secondary institutions. The three point call was actually issued after the Civil War by the Freedmen's Bureau to set goals that "would last into the twentieth century." School lunches were first subsidized in the 1940s, and the 1989 Educational Summit marked the first meeting of all 50 governors around the education agenda.

Figure 1.1 Jeopardy answers

has happened in your own lifetime, mixed with those elements that have been churning along for 250 years.

In the next section, we explore a short overview of the more recent changes in education. We lay a foundation for the current state of the profession, fueled as it is by a convergence of demands from those who have joined their voices and are moving our nation into new configurations of teaching and learning, with a specific focus on the skills that promote literacy and the making of knowledge.

Where Do Standards Come From?

We can trace the current state of education policies at least back to the Cold War and Sputnik. In 1958, responding to threats of Russia developing space-age technology, and thereby challenging the U.S. to be planetary top-dog, the federal government passed the National Defense Education Act. It focused on providing federal funding for post-secondary educational programs, focusing on science and foreign languages. The premise was two-fold: that science and research were the best path to world power, and that communicating with people from other countries would aid us in getting there and then managing them. It can be seen, arguably, as the first major federal foray into curriculum.

Fifty-five years later, we see similar aims and claims in the enormous federal grants coming through the National Science Foundation, STEM (Science, Technology, Engineering, and Mathematics) initiatives, and in the call to teach and assess "21st Century Skills" that include being able to understand and communicate effectively within different cultural systems. The link between quality education and the defense of a perceived national way of life is inferred, although now we are looking at maintaining some of our global clout and reaching out and up rather than striking back.

The second major federal change came with Elementary and Secondary Education Act (ESEA) in the mid-1960s. How was the ESEA established?

After President John F. Kennedy's death in office, President Lyndon B. Johnson continued Kennedy's legislation proposals for large-scale federal aid to initiate equality. Johnson declared a "War on Poverty" and proposed legislation aimed at ending poverty and racial injustice. One of the objectives was to improve education, in particular the education of poor and disadvantaged youths, and so the Elementary and Secondary Education Act of 1965 was formed and Title I was one of its largest programs. Title I and the ESEA would undergo fine tuning and some name changes as they were evaluated, retooled, and reauthorized periodically over the next thirty years. At the core was a commitment of federal funding to aid disadvantaged children, with the need being based philosophically on social justice and equality and driven by emerging cognitive research. However, although it had enjoyed more lives through re-authorization than your average housecat, ESEA really returned to the national spotlight when it was reconfigured and renamed No Child Left Behind (NCLB).

For many, NCLB was perceived as a major change, but it was only another step in the progression putting government into the educational makeup. In 1989, President G. H. Bush called a meeting of all fifty governors, with the focus on education reform. This National Education Summit was a landmark event, where the nation's schools were elevated on the priority list for whole-scale attention, and national goals were set. President William J. Clinton, who had been a governor at that meeting, followed it with Goals 2000, and three days into his presidency, President G. W. Bush issued a concept paper that would become NCLB. Progressively, these events established the need for academic standards, mandated that performance on these standards be assessed on a regular basis, and then that assessment results needed to demonstrate improvement, so that the nation's students were moving toward a level of proficiency that would be achieved by 2014.

So. 2014. We made many changes along the way, but 100 percent proficiency was and is magically prescribed. Our new focus is on revamping and repackaging our teaching and assessments as we respond, as a profession, to the latest point on our continuum that comes out of the collaborative efforts of governors: the Common Core Standards.

Raising the Bar: Common Core State Standards

The result of a joint effort from the National Governors Association Center for Best Practices (NGA Center) and the Council of Chief State School Officers (CCSSO), the Common Core State Standards Initiative is focused on establishing common learning expectations and goals across grade levels, so that, regardless of the state or district in which they live, students will leave high school with the skills and knowledge they need to be successful in a college and/or the world of work.

The sweeping adoption of the Common Core (44–45 states and counting since its introduction in 2010, sort of counting Alabama, which as of press time was leading a movement to secede from the standards) means that it has the momentum to make it a vehicle for real change in American schools. Whether you think it's better than sliced bread or are approaching it with caution, it's best to go to the source and know what you are talking about. According to the literature on the Common Core website (www.corestandards.org):

- The Common Core State Standards are a clear set of shared goals and expectations for what knowledge and skills will help our students succeed.
- Common standards will provide a greater opportunity to share experiences and best practices within and across states.
- Standards do not tell teachers how to teach.

While it is safe to assume that most teachers are becoming increasingly acquainted with the Common Core, the depth of their understanding and how, if at all, it translates into their classroom practices is uneven. For many of those who have been in the profession for thirty years, the Common Core is just another in a series of changes. Seasoned professionals tend to fall into two camps: those who approach the Core with all the depth of their experience and process it by comparing it and contrasting it against other changes, and those who believe that if they simply wait it out, the initiative may join its predecessors in the pedagogical pile of dead horses that have stacked up in the past three decades.

Many of the teachers at the midpoint of their careers who were already teaching when state academic standards became all the rage see the Common Core as just a second layer of anchors and elements to cite in their already-existing instructional plans. New teachers, packed and stacked with teaching strategies and tech-savvy, are hitting the ground in tandem with the Common Core, and while they are more likely to be able to assimilate it into their teaching and become native speakers, they may lack the experiences needed to contribute to its refinement in a qualified, critical sense.

No matter where you are in this progression, we are speaking to you. Whether you are a veteran educator or a novice, no one will ever be at the point where they will be able to say about teaching, "That's it. I've learned it. No need to go any further." Good teaching is a moving target, as much as what it means to practice literacy seems to change with each new handheld device. As one of the authors in this book has come to acknowledge, "We will always be this busy."

We write this text as colleagues who are committed to professional collaboration for the simple reason that we believe that it is only by sharing good ideas and pooling strengths will we have any chance of meeting the needs of our students, who bring layers of unique perspectives, skills, and perceptions to our classrooms. We write this text as experienced classroom teachers who see that real change must go deeper than pinning a standard, state-level or Common Core, on a lesson plan. We write it as professionals who like and enjoy children. Most of the other teachers we know generally do a good job navigating the red tape and actually helping their students learn. We do not support scrapping good teaching and large blocks of quality teaching time in favor of preparing kids and schools to be measured only by a high-stakes test. We do support meeting kids in the middle, with a clear idea of where we need to get them, and the awareness that there are many different paths going in that direction.

The Common Core standards set high goals for student learning and challenge teachers to support students so that they can achieve more complex levels of reading, writing, and thinking than before. These standards reflect that the needs and practices of our society have changed and will continue to do so. To be informed citizens, today's adults must be able to identify their information needs and use this recognition to propel successful search strategies, evaluate the results, and purposefully use findings in their lives. These skills must serve academic purposes and also support managing the information demands of daily life. To make instruction useful, in this sense, and to unpack the potential of the Common Core, our instruction must focus on the goal of helping students to process information through language, and it must do so in an engaging, coherent manner (Benjamin and Hugelmeyer, 2013).

(Re)Defining Literacy: Multiple Paths, Multiple Literacies

Lapp, Fisher, and Frey, in the May 2012 editor's message in NCTE's *Voices from the Middle,* ask, "Are you as 'literate' as your students?" They go on to define the term "new literacies" as "those ever-expanding literacies that one needs to navigate both personal and professional life." The definition is followed by a long list of literacy practices that are intertwined with digital technology, such as blogging and podcasting. In a way, this makes perfect sense, as written and even spoken language qualify as examples of the most basic of human inventions. From the stylus used to mark clay tablets to the ones that are intended for use on the touchscreens of handheld devices such as smartphones and iPads, technology and literacy have always bloomed from intersecting roots.

In some cases, the digital technology that we use to access and communicate information has changed with blinding speed. The idea of starting to download something on a device without having to physically plug it in (i.e., using a wireless or Wi-fi network) was a new one just a few years ago. On the other hand, email was invented way back in the early 1970s. It was created as a way to add personal commentary to data packets of information that researchers were sharing on what was then a network of a handful of servers crisscrossing the country. The network became the Internet, and both it and email became infused into how most people in the U.S. find information and communicate with one another today. So, happy forty-something birthday, you two. Sorry that you've come such a long way and are still not welcome (or working) in some classrooms.

Build on the Old, Bring in the New, Bring out Your Dead

Don Leu, the guru/top banana in studies of the intersection of literacy and technology, in a collaboratively authored article titled, *Toward a Theory of New Literacies Emerging from the Internet and Other Information and Communication Technologies* (2004), assures us that there are no completely new literacy practices, and that new literacies build on traditional ones. Consider the nicknames people choose for themselves when they set up an email account, venture into a chat room, or post on a discussion board. There are rules, both explicit and unwritten, that govern the way they use language to fit in with (or purposefully distance themselves from) a conversation on the screen. Both of these elements are actually quite similar to how people created user names or "handles" and stretched language during a fad that stemmed from CB radio use in the 1970s (Bechar-Israeli, 1998). Breaker, breaker, one-nine and cue *Smokey and the Bandit*. A lot of the perceived decay of literacy skills that our "young people have nowadays" is somewhat unfounded. Much of what happens in emails, texts, and tweets is really just an extension or progression of ways of communicating that are already in existence, such as CB slang, and these existing literacies were themselves once considered new or progressive.

What *is* new is that, after a period dominated by print, in the form of books (in schools, textbooks, and workbooks), we are now immersed in a time when, for many, the ability to get information from different places and easily communicate with others in different spaces has exploded. There are endless possibilities that go beyond just encoding and decoding messages via the tool that is the alphabet. Books themselves are no longer limited by press runs and limited editions. E-books can be downloaded in seconds and across great distances; webpages are indexed and searchable; and graphics, video, sound, and other people are all a click away. Increasingly, that click is not with a mouse but a camera. Even the American Library Association (ALA), whom you might think of as the big-muscled, staunch bodyguard of the book, acknowledges the shift in its role as archivists, noting in its 2007 Standards for the 21st-Century Learner,

> Information literacy has progressed from the simple definition of using reference resources to find information. Multiple literacies, including digital, visual, textual, and technological, have now joined information literacy as crucial skills for this century.

This progression definitely affects every aspect of living in our modern world, and because it is so pervasive, it must be a part of any classroom that is preparing students to function, thrive, and contribute in that world.

Bellanca and Brandt (2010) characterize the shift for students as a move away from manipulating predigested information in order to perform by rote on a predesigned task. The new role of the student engages them in sophisticated, authentic problem solving that requires them to effectively think, learn, work, communicate, and collaborate. In this context, learners filter data from multiple experiences in complex settings, going past one textbook version to multiple sources and mining rich layers of content. They search for information to address real-world problems and issues and do more with their answers than snap them into the five-paragraph theme.

This model requires a shift for some teachers and schools, as well. John Bransford, from the University of Washington, quoted in Bellanca and Brandt's text, *21st Century Skills*, asserts that we are still largely functioning in an outdated teaching paradigm, "In the U.S. we tell students the same thing 100 times. On the 101st time, we ask them if they remember what we told them." He calls for an upgrade, "the true test of rigor is for students to be able to look at material they've never seen before and know what to do with it" (2010, pp. xxiii–xxiv).

Change for a Paradigm(s): More Than Two Nickels

How do we make such a shift? When describing a modern paradigm, these authors begin with what seems to be a self-evident assertion: "The purpose of school is to ensure all students learn." Before you are tempted to label this as a "duh!" statement, realize it signals a significant shift in our traditional educational thinking. Traditionally, teachers have acted as transmitters of information. The transmission effects are measured bell-curve-style, meaning that a small percentage will always do well, a small percentage will always fail, and mediocrity is expected and accepted for the masses. Those who fail were viewed as having a deficit or shortcoming (sometimes related solely to being born in a family that was not English-speaking) and any additional assistance they may (or may not) get was seen through a remedial and stigmatic lens.

This perspective is changing, and in no small part due to NCLB and its push for total proficiency for all students. As unrealistic as that 100 percent goal was, it did reconfigure education so that schools needed to document that all students were progressing. We may not be capable of getting each and every child to AYP levels, but for some historically marginalized students, they are at last moving, and in a forward direction. In the professional dialogue, it is now accepted that when intervention is needed, it is not implemented from the perspective of remediating deficiencies of the student. Instead, the focus is on modifying and re-arranging the elements of instruction, including the learning environment, to best fit each learner's strengths and needs (Blanton & Wood, 2009).

A grand idea. Now we just need to move it into practice. In this way, the multi-modal worlds opened by digital technology can truly serve as an aid. In this way, lack of availability of quality technology or lack of proficiency in effectively using that technology in teaching and learning can truly be an obstacle. The 21st-century skills that are needed to manage such basic functions as healthy, economically wise grocery shopping, to the more complex issues of one's health care coverage are reflected in the skills that are reconfiguring business in this post-industrial age. We believe that good instruction must address these head on and purposefully, and yet we also openly acknowledge that "believing don't make it so."

The Best-Laid Plans

Stephens and Ballast, our colleagues at the National Writing Project, have noted that our schools are well equipped to meet the needs of the society they were created to serve . . . a society characterized by horse-drawn carriages and lit by gaslights (2011). We, the teaching professionals, are on the frontline of effecting the positive changes needed to keep up with the demands set by Common Core standards and the larger changes in society, knowledge, and technology that these standards are meant to address. We hear Lapp, Fisher, and Ivey (2012, p. 7) and nod in agreement when they assert, "'Education as usual' no longer applies," and we have infused the practices of new literacies into this work, where they are practical and warranted.

But, we have also taken steps to re-engineer the context and redesign the steps we have taken at each juncture. Real changes in pedagogy take more than just adding new devices. Stephens and Ballast assert that, "Communicating in the 21st Century inevitably leads to writing," and that the "transition from thinking about writing on paper with a pen to writing on digital ways must take center stage in teacher preparation" (2011, p. xiii). We agree, firmly.

However, this reality check is in place:

1. We recognize that not every school, classroom, teacher, or student has the open access to the Internet, updated computers, or handheld devices.
2. Good teaching without technology trumps poor teaching with ineffective bells and whistles any and every day.
3. Writing is thought on paper (National Commission on Writing, 2003). When we ask students to write, we are asking them to lay their thoughts out so that they can see what they know and think, as well as what they don't. We ask them to do research to see what other people have thought and do think, and to summarize and paraphrase so that they can remember and interact with those thoughts. We ask them to organize and revise so that they can better communicate these redacted ideas, and use them to inform a stance or argument. All of these writing activities have thinking at the core.
4. Writing is a powerful tool, for thinking and communicating, when incorporated well. Technology can add a layer to every aspect of research writing, with pyrotechnic results. Improved student learning must be at the center for both types of tools.

We have aimed this chapter toward you, the teacher, to backfill the history that brings us to this point of convergence, and to give you a solid footing from which to push off. In the following chapters, we will follow this template: a practical introduction or scenario to set up the topic, followed by a review of the literature that grounds the work in the professional dialogue. Each chapter is supported with best-practices research that explains the reasoning behind the teaching strategies and equips you, the teacher, to more knowledgeably make any adaptations needed to fit your needs and those of your students.

We've also included a snapshot of the traditional or historical means of approaching each area as well as the actual new ideas we are advocating and trying out, extensions with technology, when they aren't inherent in the new approach, and student work examples and comments.

Chapter Two: Lighting the Fire: Topic Selection with Passion and Curiosity begins with a call for change from the classroom level, starting with the experiences of one teacher, who recognized the need to do things differently in her teaching approach. The chapter provides an overview of the resulting project, the PassionQuest, and re-invented approaches to topic selection. Chapter

Three: Search and Seize: Getting to the Good Sources and Chapter Four: The Death of the Note Card? The Thoroughly Modern Research Paper, address, respectively, search and evaluation strategies, and avenues to supporting students as they read and take notes digitally. A modern approach to choosing, recording, and organizing research information is discussed, with an emphasis on how students can make progress in shaping their research findings into coherent thoughts.

Chapter Five: Speak to the Living: Real Sources, Real Audiences offers a fresh layer of researching methods that moves the process of asking questions and gathering information off of the page and into the everyday world.

Teachers often struggle with how to make quality uses of technology that can be integrated to enhance their teaching. Each chapter contains innovative teaching ideas, some of which are strongly intertwined with technology. Chapter Six: Are You Being Served? What Tech Tools to Use and Why You Should Bother provides a big-picture look at what teachers need to know in order to make knowledgeable tech choices that really fit their classrooms and teaching goals. In Chapter Seven: (D)RAFT into Unconventional Waters: Deepening Topic Perspectives and Chapter Eight: Metaphors Be with You! Organizing Connections and Building Frameworks for Comparison, we utilize two commonplace fixtures of many language arts classrooms, the RAFT (Role, Audience, Format, Topic) technique and the study of metaphors, as new vehicles for stretching and strengthening student comprehension and understanding of their topics.

Chapter Nine: The Nitty-Gritty: Cite, Write, Review, covers the actual processes of writing the draft of the paper, including topic sentences, outlining, and citations. It also demonstrates the benefits of peer review and editing, and offers clear, practical strategies for effectively incorporating these into your classroom. Chapter Ten: Beyond the Paper: Impacting Wider Audiences, explores new literacies and format alternatives that can give student learning the nudge it needs to transfer into knowledge outside of the classroom.

In this text, we have worked to offer cohesive strategies for overhauling the way that information literacy and research writing are taught in high school via the vehicle of the classroom research paper. These strategies are organized and presented as part of one cohesive project, the PassionQuest, although the individual ideas can be used as standalones within the structure of other projects you might already be successfully using.

Working on this text has allowed us to push the envelope of what we do in the classroom. We came into this project each feeling knowledgeable, but understanding that we would be learning so much more with this undertaking.

This text is the result of true professional collaboration. We have included the voices of our students, through their work samples and categories, right in the chapters. As noted, templates that can be converted for your own needs are available online and in the appendices.

We pass our efforts on to you, and your students, in your classrooms, in our big dynamic world, and begin with the experience of one teacher, from a school not so far away, in a time not that long ago. . . .

Lighting the Fire
Topic Selection with Passion and Curiosity

I'll be the first to admit it. I'm one of these English teacher nerds who LOVE teaching research. But I wasn't always. Early in my teaching career, I was given four sections of 11th-grade English to teach. Our curriculum required all of these students to complete lengthy research papers. I taught 'em everything I knew about citation and notecards and formatting styles. And then I collected all of the papers and headed home to my parents' for Easter break.

Ham and Horror

I have a very vivid memory of that particular Easter. I went to church, came home for a beautiful ham dinner, and retired to the guest bedroom to read the brilliance I was certain the papers held for me. That afternoon was one of the most horrifying and humbling experiences of my lifetime. With every paper, my will to live grew fainter and fainter. It was a mind-numbing eternity. After about three boring, lifeless papers, I had to break to eat a piece of ham just so I'd have the strength to continue. The afternoon and evening continued much like this . . . read a technically sound but boring-as-the-dickens paper on a topic with little relevance to this student, eat some ham, read another, eat a slice of pie. I probably gained ten pounds that holiday, but I gained very little in the way of teaching success.

I knew something had to change. I knew that it was possible for research to be engaging and exciting . . . even entertaining, and not just for the kids, but for me, as well. I knew I could make that happen, but how? At first, I questioned how things could have gone so horribly wrong. If it was this bad for me to read the papers, what must it have been like for the kids to struggle with writing them? I did EXACTLY what my beloved high school English teacher had done when we wrote lengthy research papers, and I got a great grade on that paper. I mean, come on! I wrote ten pages about Robert Frost's biographical information! Then, thinking back, I remembered that, despite my initial love of Frost's beautiful poetry, I was bored to tears reading about his childhood and teen years in musty old books written before even my parents could read. And by the time I actually wrote that paper, I just wanted to get it done, and done right. I wanted the "A." By the time I had finished it and turned it in, I no longer cared about Robert Frost's background.

Matters of the Matters

If I was doing all the same things that made me view research merely as a means to a grade, how could I expect my students to want more than that? I had to somehow do things differently. Over the next few years, I made many modifications to my teaching, as most teachers do the first few years out. I got my Master's in Education, focusing on children's literature, and I eventually ended up changing school districts to be a little closer to home. Early in my career, I also became involved in the National Writing Project (NWP), first as a fellow in the Invitational Summer Institute, then eventually as a co-instructor. With the Endless Mountains Writing Project, as our site is called, I had the opportunity to network with other teaching professionals in the region and nation, and participate in the type of professional community that builds on good teaching to inspire and develop *great* teaching. When great people have fun learning together, real ideas happen, and I refined and electrified a lot of my ideas about teaching writing.

It was within this professional community that I took my early pairing of passion and research, and realized that there were others interested in giving the research paper a totally modern makeover. As we began to discuss the possibilities, we all knew that we were touching on something really big. To put it simply, kids needed this. Teachers needed this. It's more important than ever that our students are able to navigate the choppy waters of the sea of information out there. But, we started out small, with Nanci and Amy coming into my classroom for a few weeks to try out different methods, and then went full bore the following year, meeting frequently to refine each step of the process and add to it. In this chapter and the ones that follow, you will hear all three of our voices, as we have negotiated and rebuilt the different steps in our work, which became known as the PassionQuest project.

In 1999, the International Reading Association called for collaboration between educational professionals and touted it as the only way we could ever even hope to adequately prepare the increasingly diverse student population for citizenship and living. Consider the ranges in background knowledge, skills, home life, experiences with technology, socioeconomic levels, access to texts, and linguistic foundations that characterize most classrooms, including differences in both the students and the teachers. Improving the communication and collaboration between experts and practitioners across different fields is not only the best answer to burgeoning diversity, it is just the next natural step forward in research in a world in which the capacity for archiving and accessing information has gone through the roof, overflowed the garage, and copiously filled rented storage space.

So almost fifteen years after IRA's call, more than thirty years into the history of the NWP, we are breathing examples of the type of professional collaboration that both emphasize, of educators coming together to share research and ideas in an effort to move teaching and student learning forward.

A foundational piece that kick-started our project came from Stephanie Harvey. In her book, *Nonfiction Matters* (1998), she writes about helping elementary and middle school students to identify passions and use them as a springboard to informational writing. Who is more adept at developing a passion than a high school student? I thought a lot about the conversations I'd had with students over my few years of teaching. I ADORED teaching juniors. They were mature enough to be able to handle some greater responsibilities and deeper conversations, and they were really discovering who they were as people at that age. They weren't relying solely on their friends' or parents' opinions to make their choices. Whether they knew it or not, they were discovering their passions. It just made sense. I connected with the Harvey book a year or so after the "Easter Incident," and utilized and modified a few of her ideas to get the ball rolling with my kids. I began to use the word "passion" so often in my classroom that year that I think my students probably suspected I was moonlighting as a soap opera actress, but it all worked.

It turns out, helping kids to discover what it is they're passionate about helps them to choose topics from which they'll want to pull every last bit of information.

Then we went further. What if we didn't only spark research engendered from passion, but research that started with inquiry and resulted in a piece that would ultimately help a student in the future? What if the product of this wasn't solely that they could write a paper with correct citations and formatting, but that they could begin to see research as a valuable skill? Meaningful research was about to make a starring debut in my classroom.

Our reimagined research project aimed at helping students identify their passions and goals and collect information and use it in a way that keeps them excited, engaged, and feeling as though the work they're doing isn't work at all, but something that is authentic and is an extension of themselves. At the same time, of course, they are learning skills that are part of the curriculum and applicable in the real world.

Hooking 'Em in Through Topic Selection

When I first started teaching, I let kids arbitrarily choose topics. It literally could not have been more arbitrary, in fact. There was a date by which students had to each commit to a topic, and typically, as I passed around the sheet of paper on which they were supposed to write down their choices, I'd get looks of terror, apathy, and general malaise. I would later read the list and be completely baffled. I got diseases, animals, serial killers, and celebrities out the proverbial wazoo. Sometimes, I'd question a student, curious about his or her choice. "Carrie, why'd you pick Muscular Dystrophy?" "I don't know." "Do you know someone who has it?" "No . . . I had to write down something!" And thus, Carrie would spend six to eight weeks learning everything she'd never wanted to know about this disorder. Additionally, often these poorly considered topics were broad, but students didn't know enough about them to find a reasonable chunk to study. Broskoske (2007) found this to be true, as well: "Students often submit ones [topics] that are too broad and lack focus" (p. 31). If I had encouraged and helped them to take time to think about and generate more meaningful topics, things could have gone differently.

When approached correctly, guiding kids to choose their own topics can be the foundation for work that is meaningful and even (dare I say it?) enjoyable. Beaton (2010) extols the virtue of self-selection in topics. "When my students choose their own topics, they become more invested in their work and care more about their writing" (p. 113). This type of self-selection adds an authenticity to task, which is important for making the concepts and the ideas last.

This Magic Moment: Beyond the "A"

Tallman and Joyce (2006) agree about the need to create research tasks that grab students' interests, "Many students may greet the announcement of a research assignment with negativity; nonetheless, if teachers can create a research experience that generates internal motivation, as well as the traditional external motivation, they will observe more permanent student learning" (p. 3). Without this kind of motivation, students will create something that may be technically correct, but personally meaningless:

> As it is now, most students quit their research as soon as they think they have fulfilled what the teacher wants. The quality of their products equals the power of external motivators, such as grades. Researching for the teacher, rather than for themselves, increases the likelihood that their new collection of facts will not generate authentic learning growth. As a result, many of the products that teachers receive at the end of a research assignment reflect students' lack of enthusiasm and motivation. (p. 3)

Additionally, they note that a disconnect is created by the "traditional" research paper process. "Frequently, these are exercises where students write about topics in which they have no personal investment, mine other people's thoughts and ideas, and reassemble information to meet the instructor's requirements" (p. xiii). Selecting a topic, in fact, is most valuable when it goes further than merely a student's interest, but satisfies a real desire for more information about an area of interest. "To be meaningfully integrated into the research process, the student's topic must arise from the student's need for information, especially information that could be useful in his/her life" (Tallman & Joyce, 2006, p. 17).

Research Is Our Way of Life, Not Just a Unit

Admit it. You Googled today. What time is your movie? Does Tony's Trattoria on 7th have calamari? What's the best way to get rid of plantar warts? Ask a high school student to Google something, and he or she will immediately, and happily, do so. This is because the research we do every day is both connected to our needs and driven by our questions. Our most basic "real world" research tasks are driven by inquiry. Our classroom ones should be, too, but we need to help students recognize the difference between quick, short-term questions and more enduring ones. They will need to recognize that enduring questions are important and relevant to them, while at the same time substantial enough to sustain their interest through extended study. Problems can arise when students don't really consider their topics and questions. "This process of topic selection means that students rarely access prior knowledge or experiences before starting their inquiry, which can lead to superficial questions that students will likely abandon when encountering difficulty in their searches" (Alvey et al., 2011, p. 141).

In our reimagined research project, an essential step is engaging students in thinking about what makes them curious. What questions do you have about your topic? What is it you want to know? Why is this topic one that you want and need to find out more about? Just as essential is giving them opportunities and support to do this sort of thinking.

Core Connections

As noted earlier, the Common Core has clearly placed research at a higher premium than have standards in the past, and with good reason ... our citizens need to be better at finding and evaluating information. Students are being asked in 7th grade to "use technology, including the Internet, to produce and publish writing and link to and cite sources, as well as to interact and collaborate with others, including linking to and citing sources" (W.7.6). They should be doing "short research projects to answer a question, drawing on several sources, and generating additional related, focused questions for further research and investigation" (W.7.7). By 8th grade, they should be self-generating their questions (W.8.7), and by high school are expected to "narrow and broaden inquiry" (W.9–10.7). The stakes have been raised, by the standards and by the world in which they were framed, and we need to be prepared to help students meet these challenges.

So How Do We Do It?

It's clear from the literature that none of us is alone in our struggle to support kids in topic selection. In Harvey's text (1998), she outlines how over several weeks or months, she helps her elementary students to discover their passions. Building on her concepts, we do it a little bit faster. Early in the year, but well before we start research, students engage in a variety of writing activities that they ultimately collect and bring together when it comes time to choose a topic.

Mommy, Where Do Topics Come From?

For the first of these activities, we call up Harvey, and write in our Writer's World Notebooks (the traditional journal times ten). If you aren't familiar with the Writer's World Notebook, check out what Ralph Fletcher (1999) has to say, and I owe thanks to EMWPer Bobbi Button, who introduced to me this now-essential element of my classroom. We fill a page with things we enjoy, know a lot about, want to know more about, and are passionate about.

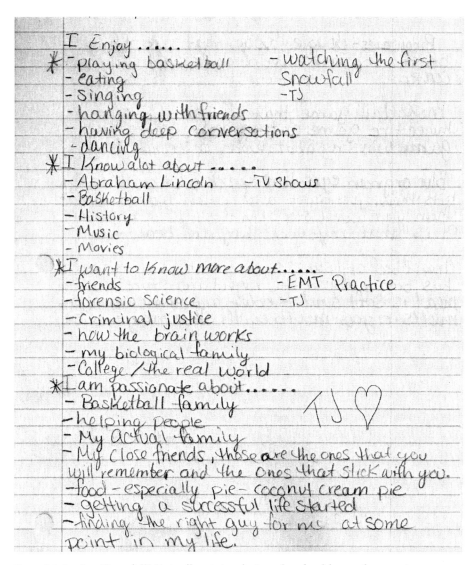

Figure 2.1 Junior Grace's "I Enjoy" activity designed to lead her to her passions

The charge is to fill the page, as students Grace (Figure 2.1) and Whitney (Figure 2.2) did here. This activity is slightly adapted from Harvey's text. She asks elementary students to categorize a list of topics they wonder about into the categories of what they enjoy, know a lot about, and want to know more about. We've added "What are you passionate about?" as again, high school is a time when many students are beginning to develop real, lifelong passions for things like a hobby, a music style, a cause, or a culture.

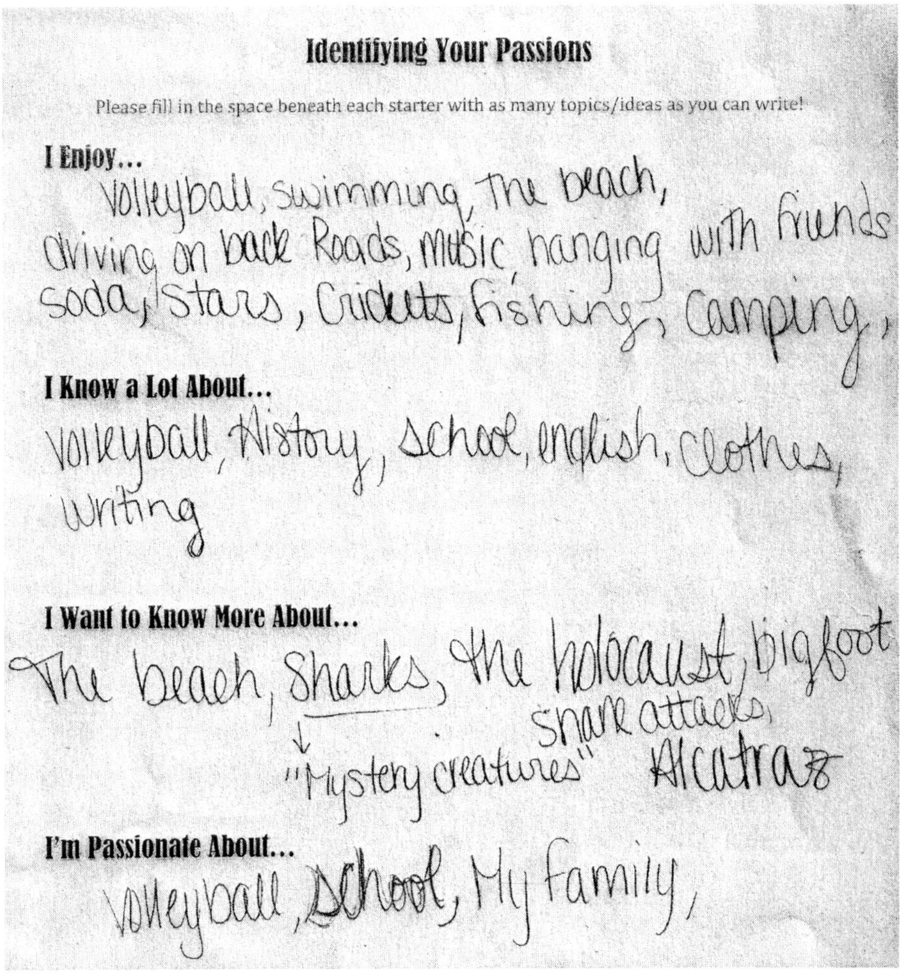

Identifying Your Passions

Please fill in the space beneath each starter with as many topics/ideas as you can write!

I Enjoy…

Volleyball, swimming, The beach, driving on back Roads, music, hanging with friends soda, stars, Crickets, fishing, Camping,

I Know a Lot About…

Volleyball, History, School, english, Clothes, writing

I Want to Know More About…

The beach, Sharks, the holocaust, bigfoot ↓ "Mystery creatures" shark attacks, Alcatraz

I'm Passionate About…

Volleyball, School, My family,

Figure 2.2 Whitney's completed "I Enjoy" activity

I've seen everything from the New York Yankees to family histories to knitting to the Holy Grail on this particular writing task. We discuss these topics and each student begins to stretch his or her research legs by doing a small assignment, like going out and finding one source about one of the topics that he or she would like to investigate. Recently, we did this in my 11th-grade Honors course. Students were excited to share the things they'd found, which included articles from the Internet about traveling to Spain, books from our school library about the history of guns, and even an interview with one student's grandmother about her family's background.

This "taste of research" aimed at helping students learn what might make a viable research topic and that when a person has questions about something, finding research is valuable and, really, pretty simple. Once we begin the "big research project," we do this activity again. Students may reference their first list, add to it, or start afresh.

Research Imitates Life

A colleague of mine (yet another EMWPer, Stacey Segur) shared with me another activity designed to get students thinking about what they are invested in. The Life Timeline assignment requires students to plot out the key moments of their lives on a timeline. The Life Timeline can be a short, two-day assignment, or can also involve some memoir writing to explore why different moments are so important and life forming, life affirming, or life changing. In addition to plotting their own life moments, students are asked to plot critical local, national, and world events they remember and consider important within their own lifetimes.

Again, reflection on these events can really enhance how students see that the events of the world that don't directly affect them do, indeed, connect them to others as a part of the world community. In this assignment, students receive a list of sample events they may wish to plot on their timelines, both personally, and as a part of events outside their personal world. Figure 2.3 shows a portion of a completed timeline from a student named Deb, who ultimately chose to research livestock showmanship. Figure 2.4 is a part of a timeline from Courtney, who investigated archery and bowhunting, and Figure 2.5 is a timeline from Alexis, who ultimately researched premature births. The timeline can serve as a powerful tool to generate a topic for genuine research inquiry. Maybe a student remembers hearing Nirvana's "Heart-Shaped Box" playing in the garage the first time he worked on a car with his dad. He knows the band doesn't make music anymore, but wants to know more. Perhaps a student remembers seeing all the *Star Wars* movies with

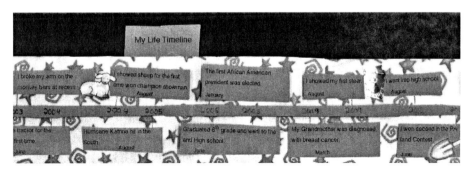

Figure 2.3 A portion of Deb's Life Timeline

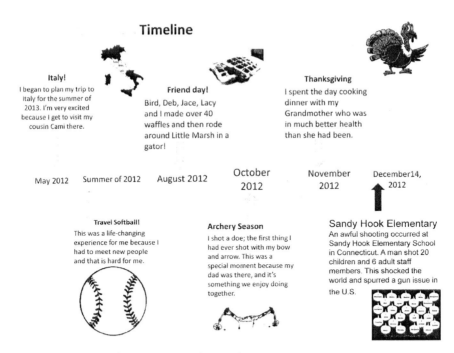

Figure 2.4 A portion of Courtney's Life Timeline

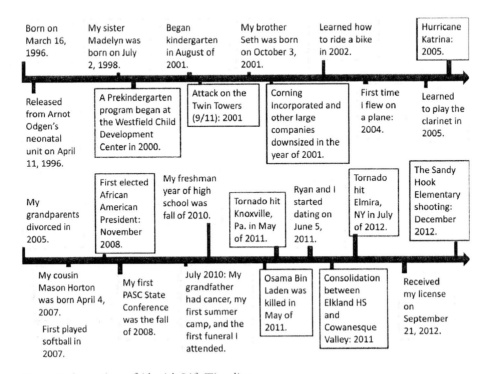

Figure 2.5 A portion of Alexis's Life Timeline

her mom, who talked about how exceptional they were for their time, and she wants to understand why.

The goal of this timeline, as is the goal of any good prewriting activity, is to spur thought and reflection, and, most important, questions. In this case, those questions can open the door for meaningful research related to a student's own life.

Superman's Not the Only One Who Can Save the World

Another way to encourage thinking about what students may be interested in investigating involves delving into the things about the world they'd like to change. This activity engages students by getting them to think about what they view to be the "big problems" of the world. Similar to the Life Timeline project, this topic selection strategy encourages students to think about the microcosm of their own world and the macrocosm of the world we all live in. The students have dubbed this activity "99 Problems," but I continue to call it "Problems of the Worlds."

Students start by drawing a small circle on a sheet of paper, and then filling it with a list of the problems or things they'd like to change in their own personal world. These might be so simple as needing more money for an upcoming trip, finding a way to succeed in algebra, or gaining confidence with the fairer sex. Next, they draw a larger circle around that one, and identify and fill it in with the problems they perceive in the school community. Perhaps there's been a recent surge of bullying in their school, or state testing has begun to be a drag (this is hypothetical, of course!). Doing an informal survey of other students or teachers is a unique, authentic way to open this discussion. My students found that many of their teachers and peers saw the same problems within our school, and that was an eye-opener. Next, they consider their communities and create the next circle about that. What problems are the families in their area facing? Having local newspapers available would be a terrific starting point for this part of the task. Finally, students consider what they believe to be the great problems of the world and nation. They may need some guidance, as the teen years can be a fairly "me-centric" time. Show them a short video about water woes in a third-world country, or one provided by Habitat for Humanity, for example.

Students really had some interesting insights about what problems existed in the world we share, and it opened up some interesting conversations. We shared a few in class, and this helped others who struggled to generate some ideas of their own.

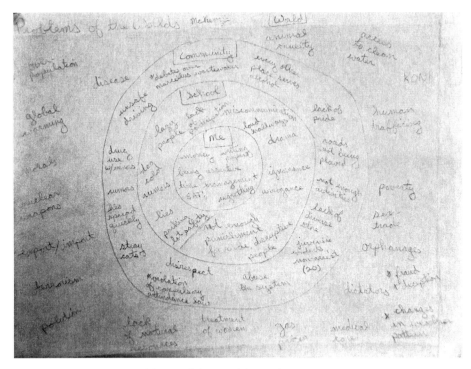

Figure 2.6 McKenzie's Problems of the Worlds graphic organizer

Figures 2.6 and 2.7 display two completed Problems of the Worlds pieces, from McKenzie and Kyle, respectively.

Another great way to develop not only an interest and inquiring minds about playing their part in the community, but also an awareness of the importance that real people place on helping out is to show your students some of the passions the adults they know have for various projects, charities, and causes. Ask teachers in your building to share with you (or, even better, with your students) the causes and charities they support. Many of our adults have traveled on a mission trip or volunteered time at a local homeless shelter or gathered items for a food pantry. Many of our school's organizations routinely work with community service. Our school's student government has worked to support St. Jude's Children's Hospital, the local animal shelter, the American Cancer Society's Relay for Life, the Salvation Army, a local food pantry, and more over the last year or so. Knowing more about what those organizations do and ways people can help is a natural fit for a student's curiosity.

For this activity, I put together a PowerPoint that featured the various causes and charities supported by our faculty members. This included mission trips to help with Hurricane Katrina, two art-based charities, some local wildlife organizations, and more. The students enjoyed hearing the causes their teachers supported.

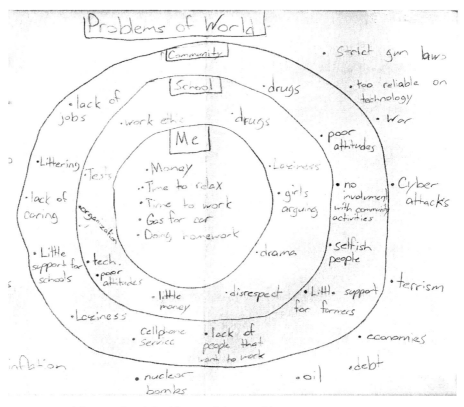

Figure 2.7 Kyle's completed Problems of the Worlds activity

Another way to spur interest and ideas is to have students explore what charitable organizations their favorite "celebrity" heroes and role models support. Guide students by showing them. This year at Christmas, for example, the news outlets were all over the story about Andre Johnson, a player for the Houston Texans, who had spent nearly $20,000 on toys for foster children. I started this activity by showing students my "heroic" celebrity, Duke Basketball Coach Mike Krzyzewski's website, on which is a list and description of the varied charities he donates time and support to. He has even formed his own. Many celebrities, in fact, have formed their own foundations to give back. Encouraging students to seek what causes are important to these adults to whom the students look up is a powerful tool for inspiring interest and a desire to learn more.

A Couple of Quick Ways to See What You Wonder About

The more ideas a student has to choose from for a research/inquiry project, the more likely the student is to ultimately choose something truly exciting and curiosity-worthy. This leads to work that is valuable and engaging.

Another quick way to see what inspires wonder is to assign kids to jot down everything they wonder about for a period of time. If you have naturally curious kids, go for twenty-four hours. If your kids haven't wondered anything since yesterday's lunch announcement, maybe try a week. You can quickly and easily make mini-notebooks by cutting paper into quarters and stapling stacks of quarter-pages together. Just today I was wondering if all the contestants on *The Bachelor* had to buy their own formal dresses, because that seems as though it could get expensive. I also saw a reference to *The Guinness Book of World Records* and wondered what records I might be able to break. These both occurred during one standard episode of a reality television show. Imagine how many hours your students spend finding things to ponder. Have you seen what they are showing on MTV? Not every musing will make a worthy research topic, but somewhere in that stack of questions might be a great nugget to use.

Another inspiration recently occurred when I looked at some of the things in my Google search history. It was quite a list of things I had wondered about! Our students Google as a part of the daily ritual of life. Do a quickwrite one day: The Last Five Things You Googled. Let them check their cell phones if they have them. Make them think about it. They might be surprised to remember what they were wondering about. Figure 2.8 shows Kyle's Googlings.

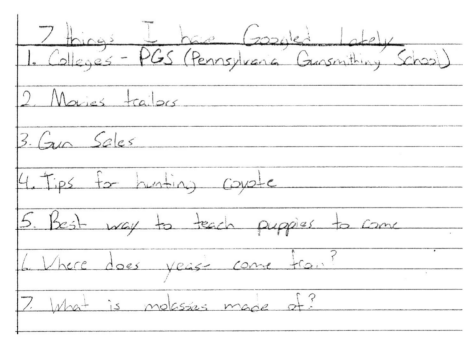

Figure 2.8 Kyle's "Last Seven Things I Googled" activity

You can sprinkle these strategies throughout the semester or school year and bring them back out when it's time to start thinking about a research topic. Students enjoy being reminded about what things they were curious about. Encourage them to add more to any of the projects, if they'd like to. We reflect on how interests change, how some things really stick, and how critical it is to ultimately choose topics that spur curiosity and a sense of wonder or excitement in you, the student. Rather than the "old school" students choosing topics from the air, you have a group of students interested in and invested in a variety of things. Help students to narrow it down to a few and begin their inquiry. When it comes time to select one for a larger project, they'll have had an opportunity to find something that will spark a natural curiosity and desire for more information as the project moves forward.

I've talked often to kids about how important it is that they choose a topic that they genuinely want to know more about, and about which they don't already think they are experts. I once had a student with a fascination for black holes. He chose it as his research topic, and surprisingly enough, he knew A LOT about this phenomenon. He was an excellent student and naturally curious young man, but he grew frustrated, because most of what he was finding was largely comprised of things he already knew. His research wasn't adding to his knowledge in a way that made research exciting and satisfying. This is why our research project begins with questions.

Question Everything

After students narrow down or choose a topic, I ask them to develop and submit a series of questions about their choice. I typically do research alongside my students, and one year I chose to research going green, a topic entirely inspired by a really interesting episode of *Oprah*. I had lots of questions. What energy-saving tricks will save me money? When, exactly, does my neighborhood recycle? What are simple tricks I could do to save energy? I've heard about green travel—what the heck is that? I'd recently attended a wedding in a green building that used toilets that didn't flush and a rainwater collection system—how does one make those alterations to a home? I let these questions guide my research. I got all the answers I desired, plus the benefit of a great deal of information that I wasn't seeking, but that broadened my knowledge and interest in the topic. Students benefit from this activity, too! Oftentimes, students will find really fascinating information that begins with seeking the answers to basic questions, as opposed to typing the topic into a search engine. Likewise, this process sometimes weeds out topics that won't be wholly engaging, as kids realize they don't really have that many questions about it. See Chapter Three for more about using questions to guide the research.

Welcome to the English Classroom. What's Your Dream?

On some occasions, I've suggested (OK, OK, required) that students investigate the steps in reaching a goal that suits their interests from the writing activity. I had a student who played baseball, but he had no idea how a person gets to be on a semi-professional team. He researched how someone might get noticed, and ultimately found a man who'd been helping high school students get recruited to continue playing sports, among other sources. Another student dreamed of one day traveling through Europe, although she wasn't sure what a trip like that cost, what places were "must-visits," and what kind of lodging was available. She'd heard about hostels, but, regrettably, had probably also heard about the horror flick *Hostel,* and wasn't sure how that might yield a positive travel experience. She researched travel in Europe, and her finished product was a very detailed itinerary for her perfect trip to Europe, complete with approximate costs and "how-tos" for each stop.

My favorite research experience as a teacher involves a very witty and boisterous student named Olivia (name changed to protect the innocent and potentially famous). She and I had spent many non-instructional hours discussing our mutual love of various movie comedies and all things *Saturday Night Live*. When it came time to choose a goal, Olivia told me she really wanted to be a comedian on *Saturday Night Live* one day. She used this as her topic, seeking answers to her questions about how someone gets an audition, how her favorite SNL stars got their breaks with Lorne Michaels, and what that actual job would entail. She did a phenomenal project. I was just as passionate as she was, I think, because I truly believed that with her wit and new knowledge, she absolutely could pull it off one day. It felt great to know that she had the information she needed to give it a shot, should she choose to do that in the future.

Those "my dream" research papers were some of the most enjoyable to read of my career. The students chose things they really wanted to do, and used the research as a means of finding out how to get there, as opposed to gathering generic information and slapping it on a page.

Topics, Topics Everywhere

The first real "assignment" for the larger research project is topic selection. After all these activities, we spend some time poring over the varied pieces of "wonderings" and "passions," and students choose two and develop the questions that will guide their research. This usually helps them to see which one will yield the most satisfying research project. Figure 2.9 shows Courtney's two potential topics and the questions she had about them.

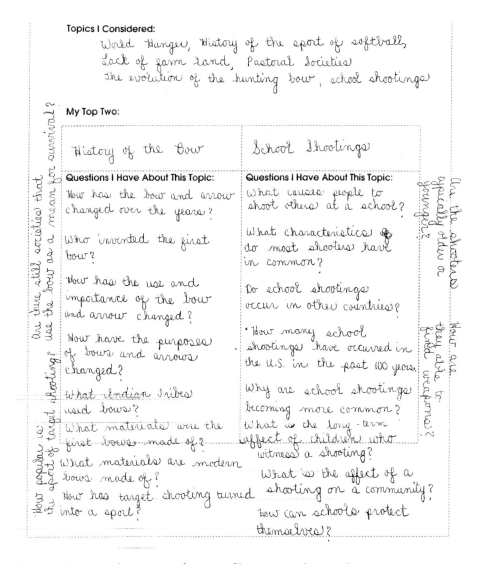

Topics I Considered:

World Hunger, History of the sport of softball, Lack of farm land, Pastoral Societies The evolution of the hunting bow, school shootings

My Top Two:

History of the Bow	School Shootings
Questions I Have About This Topic:	**Questions I Have About This Topic:**
How has the bow and arrow changed over the years?	What causes people to shoot others at a school?
Who invented the first bow?	What characteristics do most shooters have in common?
How has the use and importance of the bow and arrow changed?	Do school shootings occur in other countries?
How have the purposes of bows and arrows changed?	How many school shootings have occurred in the U.S. in the past 100 years.
What Indian tribes used bows?	Why are school shootings becoming more common?
What materials were the first bows made of?	What is the long-term affect of children who witness a shooting?
What materials are modern bows made of?	What is the affect of a shooting on a community?
How has target shooting turned into a sport?	How can schools protect themselves?

Are there still societies that use the bow as a mean for survival?

How popular is the sport of target shooting?

Are the shooters typically older or younger?

How are they able to find weapons?

Figure 2.9 Courtney's questions for two of her potential research topics

Do a Little Research, Don't Be Shy!

Initiating the early steps of research is a naturally terrifying task (What will the children DO?!), but it needn't be. Engaging students in finding the topics in their lives that warrant investigation and empowering self-selection opens the door for a rewarding experience for teacher and students. Likewise, encouraging students to purposefully seek answers to their questions as opposed to just accepting whatever information surfaces from a search engine first can be a powerful tool, as we'll see in the next chapter.

3 Search and Seize
Getting to the Good Sources

Ok . . . so you've read over your students' topic choices, and you feel pretty good. The ideas are meaningful and realistic. Some of them have even talked to you about how excited they are to learn more about their choices. It's clear they've followed their passions. Pat yourself on the back. You deserve it.

The Collaborative Process

Collaboration among teachers is essential. So is collaboration among students. Our school district uses the free Web service Edmodo to connect faculty members to one another and administration, and teachers have the opportunity to connect with students in the same way. A simplistic comparison for Edmodo is that "It's Facebook for school." (Except, of course, that it is private and secure, and the teacher control the levels of access for each student!) I was able to easily send messages to the whole class, collect assignments digitally, and leave copies of critical handouts at the ready when students left something in their lockers or were absent. While I had used Edmodo for my own organizational purposes before, this was the first time I had really used it to communicate with students and to open up a place for them to review each other's ideas online.

For students, Edmodo became a great place to share and talk about topics. Once everyone had chosen one and began the research process outlined in Chapter Four, they were required to post what their topics were and one thing they'd learned so far they didn't already know. I set ground rules, and as a result, students' comments to one another were genuine and positive. This tone helped create a community of learners, reminding kids who were apprehensive about research that they truly were all in the same boat.

The Old Card Catalog Ain't What She Used to Be

Now that they have engaging topics and they've discussed and defended them on Edmodo, the next step is to just set them free to find information, right? Finding information makes sense to us. We grew up in the library doing research in such a way that it just worked. Remember the joy of discovering the card catalog was on the computer? You probably felt a little guilty walking past the actual card catalog to try to find your book. You were sure the librarian was staring at you. You felt as if you'd been caught sticking your thumb in her apple pie. You were sure she wanted you to renounce the online version and pull out that impossibly long drawer, **"Aar–Bug."**

If I were to write a love song about my time in the library doing research in high school and college, it would include a verse on the joys of my interlibrary loan book arriving after three weeks, one on the mystery of microfiche and the skill required to string it up, and one on my bold sacrifice of laundry quarters to the hulking copy machine so I could freely highlight something in a reference book forbidden to go into circulation.

Guess what? Like a reference to the Fonz or to Richard Marx, our kids wouldn't begin to understand that song. They don't know research this way, and they don't see it this way . . . at all. Also, you've just spent weeks encouraging them to want to find out more about the things they wonder about. You've enabled their Googling. You can't turn around now and expect them to find their information like you did . . . no matter how much easier that may seem to each of us as teachers.

Think about your own recent information searches. Having recently moved to a place with outdoor space, I am interested in starting a garden for the summer but have very little concept of how that works. My dad has always gardened, and we've always enjoyed the "fruits of his labor" in the summer, but I've never paid much attention to how he does it or why he does certain things. If a certain pest shows up, he knows how to handle it. He knows when things are at just the right ripeness. He just seems to know what to do.

I wouldn't just go to Google and type in "gardening" and expect to end my time at the computer certain of how to grow a great garden. I'd get too much information, and little of it would answer the questions I already have: "What vegetables grow best in my zone?" "How do I build a raised garden bed?" "When do I need to start planting?" "What kinds of pests should I beware of, and how do I keep them out?" "What crops are ripe when?" By focusing my search on the information I feel I really need, I'm creating a process that continues to engage me beyond hitting the search button.

Keep on Inquirin' in the Real World

One summer, I took a very short, very intense course on the literature of the Civil Rights Movement. One of our ongoing assignments was to find something in each of the novels we read that we wondered about and go find more information about it to share with the group. I remember a character in one novel referencing the scent of a particular perfume, Evening in Paris. I looked it up, and sure enough, such a perfume existed. I was able to share with my classmates just what that smelled like and what the bottle would have looked like, based on old advertising for the product I found.

Another novel referenced the Woolworth counter sit-ins. I knew close to nothing about the details of this important piece of the civil rights story. I had seen one of the counters at the Smithsonian one time, but knew very little about who these people were, how they fared afterwards, and how often it occurred. I found several articles about these protests, and it really enhanced not only my understanding of the story, but also of the whole era, which enriched my experience in the course on the whole.

These mini-research tasks had everything to do with the questions I had while reading. And they lead to more questions . . . and not in an unsatisfying way, either. It made me hungry for more, and consequently, I found more . . . beyond the scope of the assignment, much to my own satisfaction.

Similarly, I've asked my students to spend time developing their questions about the literature we're studying. One year, I had a group of students that had really grabbed onto our reading of *The Things They Carried,* so we took it further. In small groups, they chose what interested them most about the time period of the novel. Students made CDs of related music, showed us grotesque but powerful photos of people affected by Agent Orange, and offered startling statistics about the number of deaths and injuries to American troops. This opportunity engaged them with the text in a whole new way. Many of those young people hadn't studied the Vietnam War in a history class and hadn't made the connections about the whole culture of the time and the ideas the speaker shares in the novel. Research is powerful stuff.

We'll get into some ways to inspire this type of inquiry and questioning later in the chapter, but we'll also get into how to evaluate the sources one does find. It's easy to seek information via a search engine like Google or

Bing, and find a wealth of information. Deciding what is valuable is another story.

Bob's Big Site of Beagle Info

The students I was teaching early in my career were still getting used to finding information in the Internet world. They loved the Internet, but many of them still didn't have it at home, and they relied on our school computers heavily for their research. My students today have greater familiarity with the Web, most using it daily to check Facebook and sports scores, but their issues with evaluating what's there remain the same. I encouraged the use of websites for my early students, but I explained repeatedly that in order to consider a website useful, they needed to be able to determine how the person who created it could be considered credible. I gave plenty of examples of reputable, valuable Web resources, and just as many examples of things to avoid.

My standard schtick is to mention "Bob's Big Site of Beagle Info" and how I could just as easily create such a website about living in Beirut and call it "Knaus's Big Site of Beirut Livin'," that talks about the pink rivers and gumdrop trees, but that I'd just be making it up. One year, I actually had a student, who, choosing to learn more about beagles, stumbled on a site from some random man who happened to really like beagles, too. It was, without being called so in actual words, Bob's Big Site of Beagle Info. The student felt the information there was really helpful and interesting, but we talked about why the site raised some red flags in terms of credibility.

Core Connections

As much as starting with questions makes sense to you and me, it also makes sense to the proverbial "powers-that-be." The Common Core suggests that as early as grade 7, students should be "conduct[ing] short research projects to answer a question . . . and generating additional related, focused questions for further research and investigation" (W.7.7). By 8th grade, students should be doing this and "self-generating" questions and using their continued questioning to "allow for multiple avenues of exploration" (W.8.7). Students will continue to build on these skills, and by grades 9 and 10, should be able to "assess the usefulness of each source in answering the research question" (W.9–10.8). This is so important to the idea of choosing the right information, not just any information you can find, that is reliable and accurate.

Guiding Your Students through Inquiry

Your students have largely chosen topics because they have wonderful "wonder-ings." Start the actual information search with these questions. I require my students to develop a list of at least five to ten questions about their topics. We do this together in class, so that I can guide students beyond the surface of the topics. For many, having successfully chosen a topic about which they truly wonder, developing questions is reasonably easy. I ask students to take this list of questions home and have a parent sign it, too, with a brief explanation of the scope of the project.

Next, I ask students to each find one, multi-layered source that helps to answer at least one of their questions. Often, Wikipedia is a great place to start this, or, should they recognize what one is, an actual encyclopedia. Don't fear the Wikipedia, teachers. It's come a long way since the "anyone can change this" days in which it dawned. What it typically contains are great starting points for further investigation, whether you choose to let students cite it as a source on its own or not. Head and Eisenberg (2009) also explored college students' use of Wikipedia in the early stages of their research tasks, "Students described Wikipedia as their 'first go-to place' because Wikipedia entries offer a 'preview' and provide 'a simple narrative that gives you a grasp.'"

When they go to Wikipedia (or a similar source) to get started, armed with their questions, students start to look for answers . . . but that's not why I want them armed with their questions. Rather, students are asked to see what other questions are spurred by this initial research, and add them to their lists of questions. These questions will ultimately guide students' research as they go, and they should grow and change as students find infor-mation. An additional benefit to starting with inquiry is that it helps to focus students right from the beginning. Again, "gardening" is a big topic; "what kinds of vegetables grow well in Northern Pennsylvania?" is more realistic and manageable.

Let students know that within the scope of your project, answering all the questions will be pretty tough, as the best research spurs more questions. This is another terrific opportunity to foster the research community of your classroom, as well. When you end the Wikipedia task, put students into small groups to share some of the questions they have and some of the questions they've already found answers to. Partners are a great resource for spurring more questions. It's satisfying to know that what you're choosing to investigate spurs questions in others, too.

Figure 3.1 shows a sample student question list from Alyssa.

The topic I am interested in researching is _The Holocaust_

Some questions I have about this topic are (you should have at least five to start this activity, but can include as many as you would like):

- What was Hitler's life before he came into power?
- What happened in the concentration camps?
- What did they do with all the people who died?
- What did they do f Nazi's who tried to rebel?
- Why blonde hair blue eyes?
- What really happened to Hitler?
- How did Hitler fall out of power?
- Why did he have people pledge to him?
   ↳ What was the pledge & what did it mean
- Was he married?
   ↳ did he have kids?
- What countries did the Jews escape to?
   ↳ were they successful
      ↳ How many?
- What did the world/other countries think about it?
- How many countries did it affect?

Figure 3.1 Alyssa's list of questions to narrow her topic from the Holocaust to Hitler's background

Is This Website OK?

Before setting kids forth to get started, it's important for you to set clear guidelines about what makes a source appropriate. Students' ideas about this are pretty interesting and may range from "everything on the Internet is true" to "as long as it's .org, it's good stuff." In order to be successful at selecting sources that will be truly valuable, students need guidance.

I am a big promoter of prewriting in my class. I always tell kids, "If you need three ideas for your paper, brainstorm ten . . . the first three to come out are rarely the three best ones you have in your brain." The same is true of finding sources. Students sometimes see interesting information and really WANT it to be true, whether there's evidence that it's credible or not. This is why it's so important they learn how to evaluate what they're finding.

My students are told to evaluate their sources, especially websites, based on criteria from the Purdue University Online Writing Lab (OWL), which goes beyond just determining credibility (which is important, of course), to include other things to look for, such as possible bias and applicability.

We take a look at some Web resources together and evaluate them based on the criteria, so we can both be sure they understand exactly what each of those questions means.

I think it's really important to give students time to get started in an environment in which they can ask questions. We usually spend a couple of class periods together in the library. I review the PowerLibrary system, a "Pennsylvania thing" that includes academic databases, a statewide interlibrary loan system, a database of previously reviewed websites, and other evaluated resources. I also remind them how to use our school district's online card catalog. Our library is small enough, too, that I spend a little time walking the stacks and seeing what is there that might be helpful. I have found that in the digital age, our students are sometimes baffled that there are actual books that are helpful in our libraries. It's always satisfying to hand off a great one to a student. They often also need a reminder about reference works.

Prior to library time, it's also important to give students resources for creating citations for their sources. I show them websites such as Diana Hacker's MLA page, and provide the old standby spiral bound MLA guides. I also try to do some kind of anti-research classroom activity to make the idea of source citation stick.

One year, my students created a movie called *MLA Man,* which featured an 11th grader in a super suit who came in to save the day for students struggling to cite a web source. He made it clear, and the movie was funny and engaging. An added bonus was the fun the students who made the video had during that process. I've also had students each take a piece of a website citation (article title, sponsor, date accessed, etc.) and physically arrange themselves in order. Both of these were simple tasks and showed students that it is acceptable to display a little creativity in research, too. Don't be afraid to think of your favorite creative classroom strategies and apply them to source citation.

The Final Word on Finding Sources

Hopefully, with your skillful and patient pedagogy, students have made it this far without getting too overwhelmed. Next comes helping them capture the information that they find and getting to a place where they can use it for their paper. In the old days, teachers could simply book the library for three weeks and not let the class emerge until they each had 100 notecards and ten written, five-paragraph pages. In today's world, they have access to more information, a higher level of expectations, and a shorter endurance for busy work. To be effective, a modern approach is definitely needed. . . .

The Death of the Note Card?
The Thoroughly Modern Research Paper

No more note cards. Toss 'em out the window and watch 'em spiral to the ground. My dad used to tell me I should take the stacks of rubber-banded note cards students turned in to me, stand at the top of the steps, and toss them down. The heaviest stacks would land at the bottom—those would be the As. The lightest packs would stay at the top, and those would be the Fs. I never did that, but I sure was tempted.

Note Cards Don't Work

No more note cards. If I close my eyes, I imagine every student from every senior English class I ever taught giving me a standing ovation for saying those words. I taught a senior graduation project unit for five separate school years, so that would be about 250 kids giving me a standing O. Back then, the senior graduation project included a ten-page, ten-source research paper on a debatable topic that utilized at least 100 note cards, a twenty-minute presentation to the student's classmates, and a presentation outside classroom walls that was appropriate to the topic. Regarding all of the work the students had to complete for the project, I'd say the single item that made kids internally (and sometimes externally) groan the loudest was the note card requirement. It didn't matter how much I tried to tell them that note cards were important tools for organization, and that note cards would give them a tactile way to sort and organize their information before putting it in their papers, even the kids who were kinesthetic learners weren't digging it. There was a reason for that, I believe.

Deep down, no matter how convincing I tried to be and how much I understood the pro-note card reasoning, I never really bought into the concept myself. I never once used them in college or graduate school. Instead, I did exactly what I didn't want my own students to do—I put colored sticky note flags all over the pages of my sources and sat in the middle of a sea of open books. I'd grab one book, type the quote I wanted from it, and put it back. Then I'd grab another and repeat the process. It was a mess. I was a mess. Note cards were supposed to be the solution, but they weren't. Why would I do the opposite of what I taught? To me, note cards seemed unnatural. Even though they weren't busy work, not at all, they managed to be busy work anyway. Why? Because they appear to be an extra step. Kids see the paper as emerging from the quotes and pieces of information, but they don't want to have to do the extra work of handwriting the quotes on cards only to type them into the paper later. Honestly, who can blame them?

Keep the Skill, Scrap the Trappings

What we shouldn't do as teachers is abandon the principles behind note cards. Students still need to organize their thoughts. They still need to organize their quotes. They still need to categorize their information into subtopics in order to develop a logical, sound argument. Whether a research paper helps students find their passions or has them arguing a position, order and logic are still required as they develop their paragraphs and include research.

In *Writing Next,* Graham and Perin note that summarization is one of the "11 elements of current writing instruction found to be effective for helping adolescent students learn to write well and to use writing as a tool for learning" (2007, p. 4). Knowing how to summarize is an important skill for anyone to have, both in and out of the world of work. I myself have been accused of not being able to do this when verbally storytelling. Therefore, I take fifteen minutes to tell a five-minute story. Fortunately, I don't have that problem when I write.

Reading for meaning, annotation, and summarization are all skills that the old-school note cards helped teach and reinforce. Students skim books and articles or Web sources to assess whether or not the sources address their topic in a meaningful way. Then, they choose the sources they think will be the most helpful. After that, they read the sources for meaning, they annotate and take notes, and then they use quotes or create summaries from the information to create note cards. From there, they create subtopics based on the information they have, write outlines, and organize the cards into subtopics. It's pretty standard research paper fare. However, students (and often teachers) don't see the benefit of the note cards. Thankfully, the same skills can be gained and put in practice with students using the very technologies they are accustomed to using every day.

Researching in the Age of the Instant Answer

Everyone searches online, especially kids. We live in the age of the instant answer. Gone are the days of kids asking parents "Why is the sky blue?" and being told, "I don't know," and having that be the end of the conversation. The same question asked of a parent today would be answered after Googling the question and finding links to many webpages, including a page on NASA's website explaining the phenomenon. When I followed Karin's example in Chapter Two of wondering what I wonder about, this afternoon alone I wondered if the style of my favorite travel dress has been discontinued (it hasn't been), if I could get an Xbox 360 with my credit card points (yes), and if that voice on the episode of Animaniacs my daughters watched was Ben Stein, the boring economics teacher in *Ferris Bueller's Day Off* (it was). Answering these questions simply required an Internet search and, lo and behold, there was the answer. The blue sky question, because it is more complex, would require more processing of information on my part so that I could provide an answer to my child. If I had to write about this question and present my work to others, I would need to record the information and where I found it, then shape it and organize it before trying to communicate it.

In the traditional method of teaching research papers, this process is accomplished with note and source cards.

- Students first create a working bibliography based on the preliminary research they've done. They do not have to use every source in the working bibliography in the final paper, and students do not have to put the bib items in alphabetical order at that time. In fact, they should put them in order of most likely to use in the paper to least likely to use in the paper, since some bib items will drop out and not be used in the final paper, but the numbering system will remain.
- Then they number the bib items 1–10 (or more).
- When they return to the sources to do in-depth research and note taking, they put each of the quotes or summaries they will use in the paper on a note card.
- They put the source number from the working bib in the upper right-hand corner of the card so that they can keep track of the source it came from as they work. Nothing is worse than not being able to use a quote because it can't be found again in the source.
- If it's a print source, students put the page number in the lower right-hand corner. If not, they use the paragraph number with a paragraph symbol.
- After doing some research, students begin drafting an outline that breaks the main topic into subtopics and breaks the subtopics into further subtopics.
- They return to their note cards and put the subtopic in the upper left-hand corner of the card.
- Then, when they are done researching, they can assign a color for each subtopic and can use colored highlighter to color the tops of the cards for easy sorting.

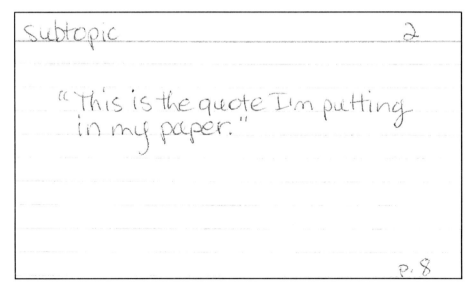

Figure 4.1 Farewell, dear note card. We won't miss you

The note card in Figure 4.1 is an example of how students took notes in the past. They solidified their outlines, organized the cards, and began the paper drafting process. Using physical cards was supposed to make it easy to move notes around into different places to make reorganizing easier. However, the drawback was that students had to carry around a big pack of note cards lashed together with a rubber band or placed in a plastic note card container. This simply did not go over well with students. You'd think you were asking some of them to chain themselves to a gorilla. Today, there is a better way.

Core Connections

The Common Core recognizes the need for students to be able to organize their research and their own thoughts and write about them. In grade 7, students are to "convey ideas, concepts, and information through the selection, organization, and analysis of relevant content" (W.7.2). Standard 4 notes that kids should be able to "produce clear and coherent writing in which the development, organization, and style are appropriate to task, purpose, and audience" (W.7.4), again citing the importance of organization. Beyond the need for producing relevant, clear writing, the Common Core also addresses the need for students to "quote or paraphrase the data and conclusions of others while avoiding plagiarism and following a standard format for citation" (W.7.8). This is exactly what note cards did, and what our source document does. The standards for 9–10 and 11–12 build on the need for these skills, adding the importance of independent "planning, revising, editing, rewriting, or trying a new approach" (W.9–10.5 and W.11–12.5), which the source document aids in doing. Finally, the source document form of note-taking helps students "synthesize multiple sources on the subject" (W.9–10.7 and W.11–12.7) and "integrate information into the text selectively to maintain the flow of ideas, avoiding plagiarism and following a standard format for citation" (W.9–10.8). The source document and plagiarism recommendations I make later in this chapter help us as teachers assist our students in meeting these standards.

The Note Card Replacement, The Source Document: This Is How We Do It

While the writing process remains mostly unchanged in the modernized research paper, using a source document instead of note cards allows students to do what they know how to do—copy and paste—in a correct way that assigns credit to the people who deserve it. Students follow a step-by-step process.

1. Instead of taking notes on note cards, students use a Word document.
2. They create a bibliography citation.
3. They create a summary for the article itself so that they can easily recall which source is which. Once sources start piling up, it's easy to forget which source said what.
4. They put all the quotes and paraphrases from that source underneath the citation and source summary.
5. After they are finished with one source, they create another document with a new bib citation, a new source summary, and then put all the quotes and paraphrases under that citation.

When they are finished citing sources, they have a rough bib and all of their cited sources already typed and in a document, so the extra step of transferring handwritten information from note cards into a typewritten Word document is eliminated. Cutting out that step also eliminates one more chance for a mistake to be made in citing the source. Then, when they write their paper, students can simply cut and paste the quote and cut and paste the citation that follows it, because both are right there in the same location. In this way, the cutting and pasting is more mindful and is done with more awareness of source. When the bibliography is due, all they need to do is format it, correct errors, and copy and paste the items into alphabetical order instead of transferring the citation information from a handwritten paper. It's so much easier, and it makes so much more sense.

Source Citation:
Catterick, Ally. "Extinction Looms for Forest Elephants." *Fauna & Flora International*. N.p., 8 Mar. 2013. Web. 12 Mar. 2013
Summary:
African Forest Elephants are on the brink of extinction. Ivory is the gold that the elephant possesses, and poachers fight to claim it all. According to some studies, scientists believe that the elephants will disappear in the next decade. Around 62 scientists took a trip to the countries of Africa and completed many observations and studies. They also wrote a paper called 'Devastating Decline in Forest Elephants in Central Africa.' The elephants seem to keep the forest living, spread the seeds and keep trails open. They are an asset to nature, and we should fight to save them.
Information:
"Study reveals 62% of all African forest elephants have been killed for their ivory over the past decade" -page 1
With the elephants dying off in Cameroon, Central African Republic, Democratic Republic of Congo, Gabon and Republic of Congo; it has been made a clear sign that they are in massive trouble. -page 1
"Saving the species requires a coordinated global effort in the countries where elephants occur, all along the ivory smuggling routes, and at the final destination in the Far East. We don't have much time," says lead author Fiona Maisels of the Wildlife Conservation Society. –page 1
Results show that the animals are moving closer to the human environment and interfering with highways, housing, and cities. –page 1
"Reducing chronic corruption and improving poor law enforcement, which facilitate poaching and trade, are crucial." –page 1
"The 62 authors of the paper – titled 'Devastating Decline in Forest Elephants in Central Africa' - represent conservationists who have worked in Central Africa with the Wildlife Conservation Society, WWF, Programme de Conservation et Utilisation Rationale des Ecosystemes Forestiers en Afrique Centrale (ECOFAC), Fauna & Flora International, Dian Fossey Gorilla Foundation International, the Jane Goodall Institute, Lukuru Foundation, Zoological Society of London, Max Planck Institute, San Diego Zoo, African Wildlife Foundation, University of Liege and University of Stirling." –page 1

Figure 4.2 Lauren's source document on elephants

If your students don't have access to the computer lab for multiple drafting days, an alternative way of doing this is the way Karin did it in her class. She created a source document handout and had students fill in their source information, a brief summary of the source, and the quotations or paraphrases that students believed they'd use in their papers.

Lauren's source document (Figure 4.2) is on the plight of the African elephant. Kasey (Figure 4.3) researched teen suicide.

When doing the note-taking itself, students used to pore through books and over webpages to find useful information, then put the information on a note card for future use. This method would still be used for books, but for

Source Citation:
NAMI. "NAMI - The National Alliance on Mental Illness." NAMI. N.p., 2013. Web. 13 Mar. 2013.
Summary:
This source is broken down into many different things about teen suicide and they are: Basic facts, Suicide signs, Teenage suicide, Causes. How to help and other serious considerations. All these will help me and you learn more about teenage suicide.
Information (be sure to include page numbers and appropriate quotation marks!):
At some point in everyone's life they will experience anxiety, sadness and despair.
"When all hope is lost some feel that suicide is the only solution."
The feelings leading to someone committing suicide are often treatable.
"In 1996, more teenagers and young adults died of suicide than from cancer, heart disease, AIDS, birth defects, stroke, pneumonia and influenza, and chronic lung disease combined."
Many of the signs of suicide go unrecognized.
There are many causes of suicide but here are some of them: major disappointment, rejection, failure, or loss such as breaking up with a boyfriend of girlfriend, failing a big exam or witnessing family turmoil.
Some of the others have a mental or a substance-related disorder and they are unable to see that life can get better and can turn around.
"Suicide is thought by some to have a genetic component, to run in families."
Suicide in a family could lead to another family member getting thoughts of harming themselves.
"Resent studies indicate that those who have attempted suicide may also have low levels of the brain chemical serotonin."
"Don't assume that people who talk about killing themselves really won't do it."
"An estimated eighty percent of all those who commit suicide give some warning of their intentions or mention their feelings to a friend or family member."
Be careful and watch for someone saying thing like, "You'll be sorry when I'm dead," or "I can't see any way out."
"One of the most common misconceptions about talking with someone who might be contemplating suicide is that bringing up the subject may make things worse, this is not true."
Don't leave a person who is thinking about committing suicide to find help on their own, they usually aren't capable.
"Most suicidal people do not want death; they want to stop the pain."
"If the threat is immediate, if your friend of loved one tells you he or she is going to commit suicide, you must act immediately."
Do not leave this person alone and do not try to argue with them.
Ask them how they plan to do it, when and where if they have a study plan and they have the materials the risk of suicide is shown.
You must take this person to a hospital or a psychiatric facility.
"Take all threats seriously—you are not betraying someone's trust by trying to keep them alive."

Figure 4.3 Kasey's source document on teen suicide

authoritative webpages, when students go to the computer lab on research days, they can sign into a free website such as Diigo and highlight the passages that they want to use as quotes or summaries in their papers. As they highlight, subtopics start to emerge so students begin sorting material into subtopic. Instead of color-coding note cards by subtopic, students can organize their highlights by making the highlight color match the subtopic the way it's color-coded in the source document. Students can put a sticky note to themselves on the page. They can create tags that can serve as tentative subtopics. Bookmarks can be rearranged by dragging and dropping. Furthermore, students can access their bookmarks and highlights from any computer, because all they have to do is log in, and there it all is. There's even an app for that for their smartphones! It's a brave new world in online researching, and students can use the skills they acquire using Diigo to do research at the college level and for the workplace. This also takes the place of note cards and gives kids a chance to use their tech-savvyness.

Note-Taking 101

To teach note-taking skills, I provided students with an informational article of average difficulty and had them take sample notes on "note cards," which was a handout with the outlines of three note cards on it. If your school subscribes to classroom sets of nonfiction or news magazines, those would be an excellent resource for this exercise. A nonfiction piece from any textbook would work, too, including pieces your students have already read. I modeled note-taking by showing them some examples of my own note-taking from the article they read, and then we all did it together in class as I projected our notes onto the screen at the front of the class. Once they had some practice with note-taking, I gave them time to take a few notes of their own. Finally, I collected their completed handouts and gave points for doing it but didn't grade it. I went over the "answers" (since note-taking can be somewhat subjective) the following day, with suggestions on how to improve what they were doing. For our purposes, a similar exercise could be done with sample note-taking in a sample source document.

When doing this exercise, it's important to explain to students that if they put information in quotation marks, it's an exact quote, which means the teacher should be able to go back to the source and find that information word-for-word. In fact, it is helpful for you to do just that with at least one direct quote from one source document per student. You could also have students in pairs search for a randomly selected direct quote in their partner's paper. Paraphrasing, on the other hand, is information that is worded differently, whether it is summarized or simply restated.

Please note that what is considered common knowledge can be more complicated than it appears. While birthdates remain the same and are generally regarded as common knowledge, what is considered common knowledge does shift. Therefore, we three authors of this book all abide by the following rule: "When in doubt, cite."

Close and Compose

One of the tips I gave students as they researched and took notes on their own was to close the book, or scroll down on the screen so they couldn't see the text anymore, and then write a summary from memory. Unless they were quoting directly, the book should not be open while they wrote a summary. In other words, they should close, and then compose. This helps kids keep from overly relying on the text itself as they write a summary. Wheeler-Toppen (2006) references Hayes's 1992 Guided Reading and Summarizing Procedure, or GRASP strategy, a strategy I was unaware of when I was teaching it roughly the same way:

> ask students to read a passage of about 1,000 words from their textbook. Then, ask students to close their books and list the information that they remember from the reading. Working with closed books ensures that students do not copy from the book. (2006, p. 48)

Pre-teaching all of this helps students see the importance in taking valuable, helpful notes the first time. It also helps them to avoid the pitfall of simply writing any old information on a note card to "get it done," which strands them in the desert of research later in the paper writing process. When the work they do is valuable the first time, they will really use that information in the paper and will be less likely to plagiarize.

Trouble with a Capital T, and That Rhymes with P, and That Stands for Plagiarism

Plagiarism is a widespread, common problem. Politicians get caught lifting parts of their speeches from other sources. High-ranking educators and officials are stripped of their PhDs years later after it is discovered that their doctoral theses were plagiarized. Students attending Ivy League universities are expelled for doing it. Why does it happen? Why do people plagiarize? Based on my experience, I feel there are two main reasons for high school plagiarism. First, it happens because plagiarism is simply easier. It means not having to do your own research and formulate your own thoughts. It means using someone else's ideas as your own so you don't have to try to sort out your own thoughts on the subject. Secondly, and I'd like to suggest more likely in the high school setting, students do it without realizing they are doing it. It's accidental, in that they quote something, forget to give credit for it, and the next thing you know, the idea is stolen. In my classroom, I showed students the importance of not plagiarizing by giving them a recent example in the news of someone expelled or fired for doing it. There is never any shortage of examples.

Truly, though, that isn't the most important reason for not plagiarizing. The most important reason, I think, is to establish the importance of the originality of ideas. Copyrights exist to establish ownership of ideas. Bitter lawsuits have been waged over the theft of ideas when those ideas have been used to create things and make money. Stealing ideas, even if only on paper, is still stealing. It is, in a sense, intellectual property, an expanding area in the field of law. Amazingly, some lawyers practice only intellectual property law, which speaks to the importance of this relatively new field.

I think it is important to teach students at the beginning of the project how to take notes correctly and how to cite sources so that students aren't tempted to plagiarize and don't even accidentally plagiarize. To me, a huge part of dealing with plagiarism is in the process of teaching the paper. That's where having them compose their paper in the computer lab and making myself available to help at all stages of the writing process is so important.

Every day, I was available to assist with any questions or problems. If no one was asking questions, I would ask the nearest student how he or she was doing. When you are there to help them at any time with any question and they know it, they don't feel as confused when they hit a stumbling block. They will ask what to do when a source isn't going to work for them after all instead of trying to wedge their foot into an ill-fitting shoe. They will ask what a passage that might be a little over their heads means. They will share their excitement about finding a book that says exactly what they were thinking about a particular subtopic. Those lab days were labor-intensive for us all. I usually lost weight from all the running around that I did. "Wow, you look slimmer. Research paper time again?"

Additionally, I collected and gave credit for working bibliographies, note cards, outlines, introductory paragraphs … every step of the process. Thankfully, by this time in the year, you've likely read quite a bit of your students' writing and can tell when the writing style doesn't match their previous work, which makes life much easier. I can recall asking a student, "What does 'cacophony' mean?" "I don't know." "What does 'metonymy' mean?" He didn't know, so I said, "But you used both of those words in your paper." I will add—with no citation. I warned him that he wasn't citing his sources, and he had to go back and find where he got those ideas and rework them into his own thoughts and opinions.

Another helpful line of questioning is the good old "how did you come up with this idea?" used in movies like *Working Girl* and *The Odd Life of Timothy*

Green. This can help kids determine who the true originator of an idea is and can help students realize that the idea is not their own. If they cannot articulate how they intellectually got from point A to point B, then it didn't happen. That path was not trod by them, so they have to go back and figure out how they got there.

A third way to help prevent plagiarism is to tell students you will check sources and then actually check sources. I'd check to see if I could find a random quote in a random source for each paper draft. When they know you'll do that and then you do it, it's amazing how kids take the paper more seriously. Kids were always saying, "Wow, you read it. I turned in a paper to Mr. P and all he did was put a check mark on it. He doesn't read our papers." I also used to use Google's advanced search feature to check on suspicious passages. It's amazing how fast and easy it is to find lifted information that way. A more comprehensive version of that is a search done on the pay website turnitin.com, but for me, Google worked fine, too.

Note-taking and Source Docs and Bibs, Oh My!

When it comes to note-taking and bibliographies, this step in the process is about students finding others who agree (or disagree) with their positions and incorporating those ideas in a logical way within one's own writing. This can be daunting for students, but it's a necessary step in the development of their writing and in their own personal growth. They must find their own voices. If they don't, they are selling themselves short. "To simply restate the position of the majority, without thinking, is to generate a report, to gather without thinking, to recopy without responding" (DeSena, 2007, p. 81). Our students have been doing reports on animals and planets and animal habitats and the Electoral College and the Bill of Rights since elementary school. They are capable of so much more, and trading physical note cards for Word and other tools they will use in the world of work is just one of the important shifts we need to help them to parlay school skills toward paying off in the real world.

In the next chapter, we'll look at how to keep this momentum going, with ideas that will maintain engagement and add layers of complexity and connection to the research process.

5 Speak to the Living
Real Sources, Real Audiences

"Go ahead, Adam, hit it with all you've got!" And he does. With a whoosh and a thud, the stick connects and the side of the piñata dissolves, showering the assembled group and grass with candy and random writing supplies. A birthday party for a child who likes to write? No ... the players are all adults ... it's just the mid-point break in our graduate-level Writing Project's summer institute.

What Hump?

Even in the most student-centered, Google-rific environment, there comes a point when both you and your researching writers need a change of pace, no matter what the age or level. We all need a little help to get over the hump. It's just part of the fabric of extended projects. In this chapter, we will revisit the question-and-search-for-answers process, with reanimating effects.

Research Takes Time

Doing good research takes time, it takes effort, and it takes a lot of brain power. Your students have likely spent hours in the library, most of them at a computer screen. They've evaluated sources and, probably, at times, been disappointed that a source that seemed really great wasn't worth its salt in credibility. How can you stave off the frustrations of the knee-deep-in-research days of your project? It may not be practical or desirable to have your high school students whack a piñata around the school yard (it usually even raises a few eyebrows on campus). But, after a few weeks of searching for sources and information and organizing what they've found there, introducing different ways to shape and extend their inquiries can breathe life back into your students. When they've grown weary of Googling and have stitched together their notes, it's time to infuse some extra jolts of energy and bring their work to life. Out with the print-only zombies, in with the living, breathing sources of information and expertise.

When our students are searching for answers in books and online, they are largely interacting with information in print form, on the page and screen. (Unless, you, as an incredibly progressive teacher, have also allowed them to include a specified amount of media excerpts and iTunesU sources, after having responsibly equipped them with the proper evaluation techniques—called "crap-detecting tools" by my students—and prepared them to take notes from such sources.) *Usually,* they end up taking notes and writing in the traditional print format, as well (although I've seen a few try to get by with taking photos of their screens or using the screen-grab command to archive a densely written page when weariness kicks in). Either way, the tasks require a lot of the same types of cognitive energy, even when the topic is compelling for them.

When our students start to lose their gumption, we have two choices. One is to, in our best efforts to stay on schedule, allow the spark we've worked to kindle to start waning in the dank world of deadlines, and encourage kids to just keep going. This sometimes happens out of necessity; no piece is ever completely finished, but deadlines and limits of 180 days are real. Another option is to regroup and rekindle. Sometimes, we can accomplish this through a brain-break activity, as represented by the piñata, or a similar divergent activity. A more extensive measure, and one that is more productive in terms of reaching your teaching objectives, is to ask the class to go back to their topics and re-examine some of the processes they used at the start, but in a new way . . .

The Same River Twice: Reading the Word and the World

Brazilian educator Paulo Freire urged us to take a broadened view of text, and stressed the necessity of becoming empowered to not only read the word but also the world that text represents, to recognize the larger ideas and forces of power that shape context and influence how ideas are connected. In *Literacy: Reading the Word and the World* (1987), Freire and (later with) co-author Don Macedo stressed the need to provide students with the opportunity to use their own reality as the basis for literacy development (p. 151). They affirmed the connections between the way we read the world and write and rewrite our own perceptions of reality, and acknowledge the role that spoken language plays in this process (p. 35), and in doing so they laid a foundation on which teachers of adolescent literacy have since built their practice.

Based on Freire's pioneering work in creating the field of critical literacy, language arts teachers (and sometimes even those in social studies!) today understand literacy to be social and contextual. We work within a constructivist stance that recognizes that when we are all looking at the same words on the page, the ways that each reader perceives and connects to them is inherently rooted in their own experiences and beliefs. This same variance applies to events and happenings, both great and small, in the world. Consider your teenage neighbor with the pants waist riding low, the backwards ball cap, and the obscenity-strewn music blasting out of his pumped-up pickup truck. In his mind, he looks GOOD and thinks everyone is so in tune with his musical selections that they rejoice in the chance to jam along for the few moments on the sidewalk as he powers by. And to many in his peer group, this perception is correct. If he is pulling in for a job interview, the perception of those at his destination will likely be much different. If he is arriving to conduct an interview with a Holocaust survivor to get information for his PassionQuest project, again, the perceiving audience is different. Same facts, different interpretations.

Recognizing that there are reasons for differences between how people act and interact is a prerequisite to building a society where tolerance is based on an understanding of diversity, rather than just on how much difference you can put up with. This recognition is also at the root of qualitative research and naturalistic study, fields that seek to develop perspective on and make meaning from events and facts, which, in essence, is what we are asking our students to do when we ask them to read, to research, and to make connections through writing.

Luke and Woods (2009) note that, "Critical literacy provides a way for teachers and students to 'reconnect literacy with everyday life and with an education that entails debate, argument, and action over social, cultural, and economic issues that matter'" (cited in Damico & Baildon, 2011, p. 234). They stress that access to information and ideas through technology means that "people are more aware of the local and global interconnectedness of issues related to, for example, health, nutrition, poverty, the environmental impact of pollution, racial and gender injustices, immigration, and climate change."

And yet . . . sometimes we get so caught up in priming students to ferret out quality text sources that we forget that they had living, breathing authors, people who were knowledgeable on the topic and wrote about it. And these people, or people like them, exist in the world today. Some of them are local, and others can be reached via phone calls, emails, or Skype. Preparing our students to contact these potential resources requires thought and advance planning, so that the results are meaningful and so that students do not make a poor impression of themselves in the outside world.

Opening at the Close

In the early stages of topic selection for our project, students mapped out "Problems of the Worlds" and brainstormed issues on four levels: in their personal lives, at the school level, community level, and then at the national or global scope. We ask them to return to the four levels in the "Problems" exercise, this time not for the purpose of identifying topics, but to identify resources at each level, specifically resources in the form of living, breathing people who have information and opinions on their topics. We ask them to bring the same type of judgment they used to decide if the author of a website is credible to identifying believable, quality people that they can interview and email, and actually converse with. Students can also, at this stage, find out what others know about their topics so that they can begin to direct their findings toward their future audiences.

This activity reawakens the inquiry spirit and brings the research process around full circle. It acknowledges that the sources we have been reading are just one format in which voices can be shared, and helps them to transfer over their inquiry skills into the larger world.

The first time we incorporated the "Speak to the Living" part of the research task, it was after the students had already completed the research paper. The teaching focus at that time was to see if, having already become knowledgeable on their topic and having already produced a paper on it, the students would be better-prepared to approach an expert, ask deep and meaningful questions, and be better able to hold their own and contribute to the resulting discussion. Could we push them to take their knowledge and communication to a more complex level of thinking? Once we started this phase of the project, we realized that not only was the answer to that question a resounding "yes!" but that the approach also had some rejuvenation powers that we had not fully realized before. Or, to quote Karin's email after the first day in the classroom with this phase of our project, "ABSOLUTELY awesome start to Speak to the Living. SICK and CRAZY AWESOME ideas abound from these kids. It was a good day." With feedback of this magnitude, we knew this was a powerful addition to our research renovations.

Core Connections

Speaking to the Living not only invigorates the process of research for students, but it also offers them a chance to use their skill at evaluating sources in a different way. Higher-order thinking skills DEFINITELY required! Couple this with the real-life skills students gain by preparing for an interview, developing effective questions, and speaking to someone in this way, and this piece of the research project is tough to argue against. In fact, the Common Core Standards suggest that students "integrate multiple sources of information presented in diverse media or formats (e.g., visually, quantitatively, orally) evaluating the credibility and accuracy of each source." Students need to be able to see possible bias in people and know how current their information is, just as they would another source. Likewise, they have to figure out how to integrate this new resource with the others they've spent time gathering. A thinker, for sure. Finally, students need to be able to use this information to help address the remaining questions they have or solve an issue. Says the Common Core, students should, "Integrate and evaluate multiple sources of information presented in diverse formats and media (e.g., visually, quantitatively, as well as in words) in order to address a question or solve a problem."

Talking 'Bout a Revolution

To get started, students circled back to their four worlds organizer (as outlined in Chapter Two: Lighting the Fire: Topic Selection with Passion and Curiosity) and used it as a jumping off point for a new graphic organizer. Their new work still required them to make a series of concentric circles, but this time, they filled each circle with people or groups of people they might speak with to gain more information on their topics. For some students, this was a quick process, and they decided right away to whom they wanted to speak. For others, it proved to be quite a challenge.

Working together, we identified some really exciting connections. For many of the students, the focus was on seeking out a specific individual. Others decided that creating a survey of many people would give them information that would help them to better understand what was already "common knowledge" or "common perception" about their topic. These responses yielded some interesting comments that many used in their work later on.

Before venturing outside of the classroom, we set ground rules. Some students knew someone already who might add insight on their topic. Others chose strangers to contact, like the young man who contacted the son of a friend of mine, whom I had never met. He had sparred with the UFC fighter my student had researched. In a case like this, it's better for the teacher and student to work in tandem to set up the contact. For obvious reasons, we have a class-wide discussion about Internet safety, and your role as a teacher is to serve as a go-between for students sending these kinds of cold emails. Students devise their questions, and they are sent from the teacher's school email to both add a layer of legitimacy to the request, and to protect students' privacy.

Another important layer of groundwork for Speak to the Living is a lesson on devising quality questions for an interview or a survey. We discussed the concept of "fat" questions, those that yield rich, detailed responses, as opposed to yes/no, "skinny" one-word answers. Each student works to create several "fat" questions about their topic in guided practice and has to get them approved before using them. The students also have to identify what they are hoping to gain from their interviews or surveys, and speculate on how they think they might use that information later on as a means of directing the types of questions they asked.

Figure 5.1 shows the fat questions student Lydia used when gaining insight from two sources on her topic, human trafficking. The first set of questions was sent to a friend of Lydia's who was living in Thailand, an area in which human trafficking is prevalent. The second set of questions are from Lydia's contact with a woman in a nearby town who has a retreat for people rescued from human trafficking.

Figure 5.2 displays Anthony's questions of Vincent Nance, a former MMA fighter who had sparred with Jon Jones, the fighter Anthony researched. Figure 5.3 shows one of Vince's rich answers to Anthony's questions.

We also work in groups to identify appropriate behaviors for requesting information, sitting down for an interview, and administering a face-to-face survey. The students direct this process, with teacher guidance, to ensure we talk about such things as:

- Dressing appropriately
- Being prepared with questions, writing utensils, and paper
- Remembering that people are giving their time to help, and so treating them with gratitude
- Using appropriate eye contact
- Exhibiting good manners
- Providing your resources with a little background information about what you've already learned, so that they aren't repeating things you don't need and wasting valuable time for both of you
- Speaking clearly and confidently
- Sharing how you plan to use the information they give you

Students who have done interviews have typically had a lot of success. One, interested in animal abuse and perhaps becoming a humane society police officer, interviewed a local veterinarian about the abuse cases she sees. She had a variety of national and international statistics in her research, and the local information she learned from this source provided perspective on how the problem affects us locally. Another student, who had researched Nike, contacted the owner of a local shoe store, who in turn drew on her experiences to explain why she felt people buy Nike and how popular it is in comparison

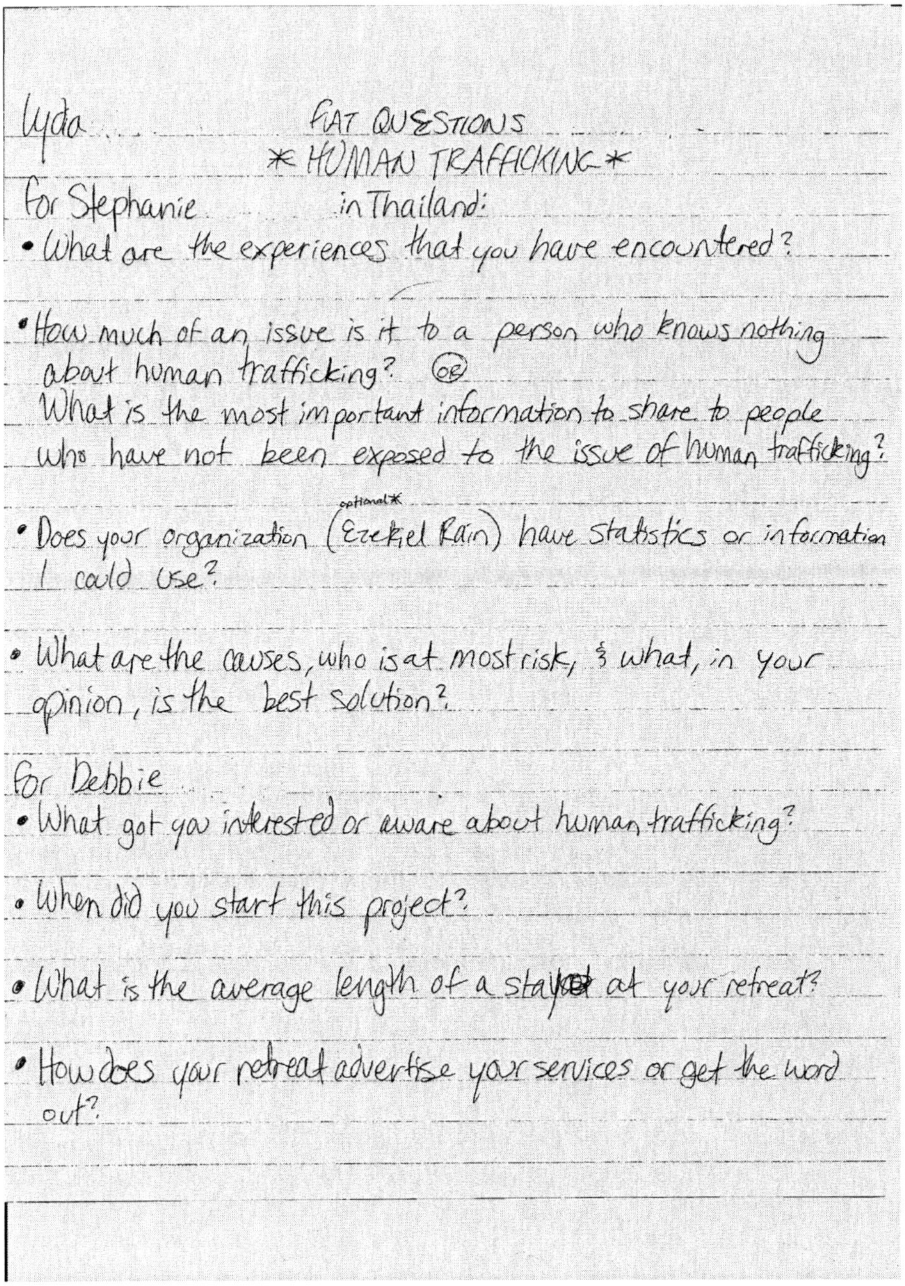

Lyda   FAT QUESTIONS
                    * HUMAN TRAFFICKING *
for Stephanie   in Thailand:
• What are the experiences that you have encountered?

• How much of an issue is it to a person who knows nothing
  about human trafficking? ☺
  What is the most important information to share to people
  who have not been exposed to the issue of human trafficking?

• Does your organization (Ezekiel Rain) have statistics or information
  I could use?

• What are the causes, who is at most risk, & what, in your
  opinion, is the best solution?

for Debbie
• What got you interested or aware about human trafficking?

• When did you start this project?

• What is the average length of a stay at your retreat?

• How does your retreat advertise your services or get the word
  out?

Figure 5.1 Lydia used these "Fat Questions" to gain more information from two people who had insight on human trafficking

Karin Knaus

Sent: Monday, April 29, 2013 8:05 AM
To:

Terrific! He's obviously interested in your insight on Jon Jones, but he also would enjoy and benefit from any insight you have into the UFC and MMA.

How did you get into MMA?

At what level did you fight?

Are you still fighting?

What was it like sparring with one of the greatest fighters in the UFC?

How did you come about getting the chance to spar with Jon Jones? Were you excited when you found out?

How did you do?

Did he teach you anything you didn't already know?

Do you look up to him as a fighter? Does he have an influence on you?

How many times did you spar with him, and for how long?

Did you guys talk outside of the cage? Do you have a relationship outside of the fight?

Have you ever watched him at a real UFC event?

What were his attitude and personality like?

Many, many thanks!

Karin

Figure 5.2 Anthony's "Fat Questions" for Vincent Nance, who sparred with the MMA fighter Anthony researched

4. What was it like sparring with one of the greatest fighters in the UFC?

Answer: We fought in the fall of 2008, and at the time, he was scheduled to make his debut in the UFC against Stephan Bonnar around January, 2009, I think. But it was still painful! It was pretty casual at first, with him not really trying anything crazy, testing me out and using his reach advantage. Then he switched his feet twice in less than a second, making me look down at them to figure out whether he was south paw or still fighting right handed, and jumped up straight at me with a flying superman punch to my forehead. I saw stars hard, and it sent me straight back against the cage, bouncing me back at him for the last minute or so of sparring, but I realized then that his level was much higher than I had expected. Kept my hands up and fought defensively for the rest of the round. I didn't know his name before the round, and never forgot it after - I called him as being the next UFC light heavyweight champion before he had even set foot in a UFC cage, because of his athleticism and creativity. It was like watching a tiger play with dogs.

Figure 5.3 Vincent's rich answer to one of Anthony's "Fat Questions"

to other brands she sells. Finally, Lydia, whose questions appear in Figure 5.1, who investigated human trafficking, was able to speak to an acquaintance living and working in Thailand, a person who had a global perception of the idea from one of the areas in the world in which human trafficking is at its worst. Additionally, she was able to speak to the operator of a retreat for girls rescued from human trafficking which exists just a few towns over from ours. It was powerful for her, and later on, when she shared what she'd learned with the class, her peers were able to see how this international problem which doesn't affect them day-to-day hits closer to home than they realized.

When a source is far away geographically, it's still possible to bring their voice into the project, whether by means of telephone, email, or, increasingly, through online video services such as Skype. While we utilized face-to-face communication, the telephone, and email for the project this time around, it is likely that in the future we will have more options open for this purpose and will be able to incorporate more real-time multimedia connections.

Students interested in creating surveys can benefit from reviewing the basics of the Internet service *Survey Monkey. Survey Monkey* allows an individual to choose from a variety of formats and sentence stems to create a survey of up to ten different questions. When reviewing the different options, the students really get a feel for the different ways to craft a question and the answer choices so that the results are returned in useful formats. A lot of small companies and professional groups utilize *Survey Monkey,* and for students to have a familiarity with the way a survey is constructed can help them to be more critical when they themselves are on the receiving end of a survey request or see results of a survey reported in the news or a publication.

When our faculty is their desired focus group for their questions, the links to the online surveys can be sent through the school email system for distribution. Other students have shared their surveys on Facebook or have printed paper surveys to hand out in class or at lunch. One student interested in traveling to Africa focused her survey on commonplace conceptions of Africa, and she posed her questions to a middle school world cultures class, with a goal of later sharing with them some of the information she found that might change some of the *mis*conceptions they had about the area. She shared those ultimately with our high school class instead.

Students used their survey results for varied purposes. One student who investigated the history of video games surveyed just five people, all teachers of "different generations." He asked what video games were popular when they were growing up, how much a person paid for a game, and whether or not they thought that was worth the price, among other questions. He was able to use this information to supplement what he'd learned about the progression of video games, adding a more personal perspective to the timeline.

There are endless connections for students to make between their topics and their worlds. Figure 5.4 shows some samples of topics and connections students have attempted before, designed to illustrate the kinds of connections you can help students make for themselves.

In this chapter, we've explored ways to use face-to-face communication and technology for connecting with real-life people and the different types

Personal World		School World		Community World		Global World	
Topic	Living Resource	Topic	Living Resource	Topic	Living Resource	Topic	Living Resource
Leukemia	Her mother, whose sister had the disease	The effects of "hard drugs"	The school's probation officer, who talked about prevalence in the area	Obsessive-Compulsive Disorder	A local therapist	Animal abuse	Reporters of stories she read for her research
Livestock showmanship	Leader of her 4-H group	End of Olympic wrestling	High school wrestling coaches	Nike	Local shoe store owner	Human Trafficking	Person who runs a retreat for rescued girls
Canine Therapy	A friend who is studying to do canine therapy	Trapping	A science teacher who is a trapper	How to become a journalist	A local college professor of journalism	A favorite UFC fighter	An MMA fighter with local ties
Gun laws	A relative who is a gunsmith	Teen Suicide Prevention	Classmates, on what they know about signs and solutions				

Figure 5.4 This table illustrates some of the connections students have considered and even attempted to make with outside, human sources

of knowledge they had to offer. In essence, we've helped students develop their voices and better listen to the voices and perspectives of others. We've explored how services and devices such as the telephone, email, and *Survey Monkey* can extend students' circles of communication and their possibilities for researching. In the next chapter, we'll look a little more deeply into the relationships between technology and literacy and how we can knowledgeably choose digital tools to enhance all the aspects of the researching, writing, and sharing phases of your research project.

Are You Being Served?
What Tech Tools to Use and Why You Should Bother

This chapter is in the middle of the book for two reasons. First, some of your students use technology extensively and some do not. Those that are "wired" don't necessarily use their powers for their own academic good, and there are those who will need to be drawn into it. Both groups will need support in becoming savvy with digital information and communication. Regardless of where they are with technology, they are not yet where they need to be with the thinking and communication skills they must have to function in the world as informed and contributing adults. You need to make an effort to meet them in the middle so that you can move them forward.

The second reason: in Chapter One: All That Rises: Convergence Drives Change, we stressed the impact of technology on redefining literacy and addressed new literacies. In the other preceding chapters, we've established the potential of Google's search engine and Wikipedia for helping students to find information, and Microsoft Word and Diigo for supporting the transactional process of making meaning from information through digital note-taking. We've also mentioned and discussed Edmodo as a tool to spur communication while the work is underway. Later, in Chapter Ten: Beyond the Paper: Impacting Wider Audiences, we'll provide some examples of what you and your students can do with tools that have been designed (and co-opted) for presentation of final projects.

In this chapter, the goal is to provide you with an overview of how tech tools intersect with literacy, so that you can make better decisions about what tool or tools to purposefully use with your students to get them to that final stage. It should get you thinking about what you already do and what you want to do, and how technology can assist in both areas. If there are there still obstacles in your way, and perhaps some reluctance on your part to utilize technology with your students, this chapter should help you to better recognize the bigger issues and possibly nudge you toward trying out something new. If you are already comfortable using tech tools in your teaching, we hope you will still gain some new perspectives from our approach. By the time you are done with this chapter, we hope to spark something that wasn't there before.

Are You a "Techie"?

Where might you fall on the continuum in Figure 6.1, Loose Continuum of Teaching with Technology? It depicts different stages in classroom technology use and the shift from traditional "telling" or transmission-based teaching to more collaborative and digital means.

The Pew Internet and American Life Project (2013) has a separate category for what I like to think of as "techies." That category is defined as "FOUR-OR-MORE: an exceptionally connected early adopter group of those who own four or more Internet-connected devices." I'm guessing that an unwritten part of this definition is the caveat: owns *and actively uses* these four-or-more. A lot of American adults have two or more cellphones that are registered to them and may technically own multiple iPad/tablet and gaming devices but use *none* of them, due to having one or more children (or gamer spouse) in the household. If you are such a person, you know firsthand what I am talking about. I have personally beheld a group of four ten-year-old girls sitting at the same table, silently, speedily, deftly texting to one another without a hint of eye contact or vocal motion (OMG! ★shudder★). None of these young ladies would share her device without a fight, even if it were with the parental figure who had purchased it and had taken on a side job to pay for the data plan. Keep calm and carry on, but don't touch my handheld!

If you are not a techie according to the Pew definition, consider the most opposite end of the spectrum. Most people who talk and read frequently about technology know the term "Luddite," which Jones has defined as "one who has extreme hostility toward technology and progress" (2012). In everyday use, the technology resistance is the part of the definition that is most commonly invoked, and then almost always in reference to technology that is digital. If we went strictly by this definition, an absolute Luddite would eschew shoes, clothing, and even human language. If we went by a strictly historical context, we would acknowledge that the term allegedly originated in the early 1800s, as a textile worker named Ned Ludd inspired imitators who destroyed automated

Me Luddite. You go away.	Ugh...not me! I do fine with paper, pen, and overheads.	Well, I have upgraded most of my VHS to DVD, and I project these on my Promethean.	I've made PowerPoints and some multimedia projects for my classes.	I update grades and assignments online regularly through my school, and for students and parents.	My classroom is essentially paperless; my students conference online, turn in multimedia work digitally, and I provide feedback that way as well.	Bazinga! We muddle in the Moodle, NoodleTool our knowledge, and my students are informational writing superstars!

Figure 6.1 Loose continuum of teaching with technology

cloth-making machinery. As with most terms, though, we tend transfer only part of the full meaning; in this case, "I hate technology," really means, "Don't ask me to use that device. I don't want to and you shouldn't try to make me." Recognize anyone on your faculty here? No shoes, no shirts, no cell service.

Often, what accounts for the difference between classrooms where students use technology to gain real ground and those that don't is a reflection of the comfort level and pedagogical stance of the teacher. Sometimes, district policy makers make interesting decisions about blocking HotMail, YouTube, and even Google from school servers, throwing a wrench into teacher plans and visions. In some cases, technology is not integrated because it's not yet available in a school. In all/any of these cases, teachers are the ones on the front line. Whether you are looking at making changes in your own teaching, trying to change district policies, or raising funds for equipment and services, you will only be successful if you can fully support *why* anything should be done differently. To do that, it's helpful to be looking at a bigger picture.

Tech One, Tech Two

Technology, by definition, refers to any tool that is created or designed to serve a specific purpose. The operative word here is "designed," as opposed to anything that is already in existence in nature and is "discovered" by someone. Teachers and students are surrounded by such tools, but understanding them and being purpose-driven about when we choose to use them is the challenge.

Tools that affect modern teaching and learning, in particular tools related to how we perceive and serve the objectives of the modern research paper, can be categorized according to the broader terms of the purpose they serve. In this discussion, we are focusing on technology used for these purposes:

- Providing storage for and access to **I**nformation
- Facilitating human **C**ommunication (both intra- and interpersonal)

If this two-pronged concept seems a little cumbersome, well, there's a mnemonic for it. "**ICT**" stands for "**I**nformation **C**ommunication **T**echnology," and the term can refer to modern digital technology or older, analog-based inventions such as the written alphabet, stylus, typewriter, etc., depending on who you are talking to and their understanding of the term. So, yes again, it's reflective of your own personal and professional context, though not always of your generation.

Try making a list of devices that would qualify under this definition. Use the margins or endpapers, and give yourself five to ten minutes. (Feel free to try this at a staff meeting. I wouldn't suggest it for a party game, unless it's a pre-Star Trek Episode 12.4-release type of affair.)

When I use this activity in a class or workshop, I typically ask participants to go back to their lists and pick what they feel are the most important ICTs in human history by ranking them in terms of impact. Often, I'll ask them to choose the top two and write them on a group list, with no repeat additions allowed. If you try this activity with a group, you usually will end up with an expansive list spanning digital and analog devices, which serves to activate or frontload thinking about the larger role technology has made in shaping how humans access and share knowledge. For example, Figure 6.2 Compiled ICTs List, is an example of what was posted after a small group of participants had brainstormed and then posted what had ranked as their topic choices.

Think about which of the listed devices have directly and heavily influenced your own learning, and then also your teaching practices. Then delve a little more into why you chose to use or ended up using a device or service. Take stock of all the technology that has already come and morphed, and you will be less awestruck (i.e., dumbfounded) by what's ahead. You'll also start to recognize the progression that connects traditional and "new" practices, a progression noted in Chapter One: All That Rises: Convergence Drives Change.

You can also modify this approach to use with your students to get them looking at where they are with technology and how they got there. (Most modern literature anthologies have at least one good science fiction story to springboard them into this type of discussion, if you need a stronger curricular tie-in.)

Why is it important to establish perspective ourselves and then help our students to do the same? Because some of them, like some of your colleagues, are digitally wired to the teeth, and others, well, if it weren't for school access,

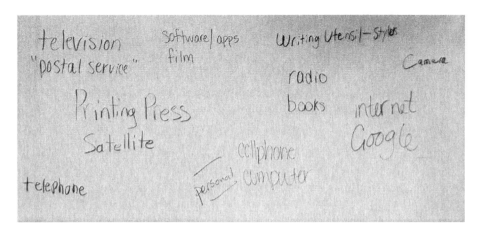

Figure 6.2 Compiled ICTs list

then they'd have no net at all. Because they, like you, are trying to make their way in an information-drenched, device-heavy world, and have different ideas about how and where to look for answers. The devices we know and use in our classes will be replaced by different tools in the future, possibly even before the end of the year, but building this continuum perspective prepares us to understand this process and critically evaluate services as they become available.

As a teacher, your tech choices should be guided by these bigger ideas of using tools with the purposes of locating and communicating information. Specific choices would be shaped by your curricular goals (if your focus includes using more scholarly sources, you might stick with a service like the previously mentioned PowerLibrary, for example), and availability. Keeping the larger processes of what you are trying to accomplish in mind can really help you make the most effective decisions.

Figure 6.3, Tech Services and Apps, provides a chart of just some of the tech tools that are currently available and in use in classrooms today, categorized by their functions and potential for classroom research projects. Please note that just as literacy practices and measures change, services and devices do, as well. This chart is provided as your departure point and was current when this text went to press.

Each service is coded with an I or C, depending on where it can be used in the research process; to find Information and then Communicate the completed work. It should be noted, however, that with the recursive nature of the research and writing process, some of the services have potential in multiple ways.

As noted in Chapter Four: The-Death of the Note Card? The Thoroughly Modern Research Paper, there are important steps between finding information and then presenting it. Presenting it unchanged and uncited is the very definition of plagiarism. Adding the citations may make the work street legal but still a cheap copy. Our students can use many of the communication tools to archive and organize information for themselves (intra-personal communication) in rich and complex formats, and to share findings and draft ideas and sequences with partners when they are working collaboratively or exchanging feedback and craft their final pieces (interpersonal communication).

Another aspect that might be considered prior to viewing the services sites characterized as having "I" potential is that they are best understood as examples of "Web 2.0" technology. To understand Web 2.0 technology, consider that "back in the day," you got online and searched for information via a search engine. The inter-connectivity and social networking aspects of Web 2.0 services essentially can turn this action on its head. Social networking services allow you to read online information, and to share and comment on it. Many services, however, also allow you to tag/categorize content (as we saw with Diigo) and then also to see what else a particular author or poster of content has published online. The

Stage	Service	What does it do?	Teacher Accounts	'Following' feature	'Sharing'	iPad Accessibility	If you like this then you might like...
I	Scoop.it	Allows users to collect and create short annotations for content from the web in one place. Users can also browse content generated by other users, follow topics or users, or view recommendations from Scoop.it tailored specifically to that user's interest. URL: www.scoop.it	N	Y	Y	APP	Pearltrees (pearltrees.com) Pinterest (Pinterest.com)
I	Pocket Formerly called *Read it Later*	The Reader allows users to bookmark websites, articles, blogs, posts, tweets, etc., in one central location. This is different from traditional readers because it allows users to store posts and tweets from web pages that change by the minute. URL: www.getpocket.com	N	N	Y	APP	Google Reader (www.google.com/reader) Paper.li (www.paper.li) Storify (www.storify.com)
C	NoodleTools	This is not just a great citation generator; Noodletools also contains a notecards feature that allows users to create and organize notecards, linking them to citations. The notecards can also be exported as an outline. URL: www.noodletools.com	Y	N	Y	WEB	Bubbl.us (www.bubbl.us) – a site for brainstorming and creating graphic organizers
C	Google Drives Formerly called *Google Docs*	Create presentations, documents, forms, and spreadsheets online. These items can be collaborative, with multiple users editing the same document at the same time. Google Drives allows users to leave comments on content and real-time chat with other document users. All items can be downloaded and saved to the hard drive in a variety of different formats. URL: www.google.com/drive	Y	N	Y	APP	Microsoft SkyDrive (skydrive.live.com) Drop Box (www.dropbox.com)
C	Voice Threads	Users can post original content or comment on topics added by other users. Comments can be audio or video clips, or text, and users can also add notation directly to the slides while commenting. URL: www.voicethread.com	Y	Y	Y	APP	No comparison... it's multi-media-riffic!
C	ThingLink	Users can import images and create a layer of annotations on the image. Annotations are made in the form of small buttons or tags. Annotations can include text, links to other web content, additional photos, or video. URL: www.thinglink.com	Y	Y	Y	WEB	Also a unique tool, although the annotative layer is similar to that of Diigo.
C	Wikispaces	Users can create personalized multipage websites that display a variety of web and user generated content. Wiki users can link or embed media and other web content to their pages or upload their own documents and files. URL: www.wikispaces.com	Y	N	Y	WEB	LiveBinders (www.livebinders.com)

Figure 6.3 Tech services and apps

C	Wordpress	This blogging site allows users to analyze information found or experienced, then create new web content form their interactions with information. This blog allows users to insert media, post, and link concepts to existing web content via hyperlinks. Wordpress users can generate stagnant pages as well as dynamic blogging pages, making the site even more versatile. URL: www.wordpress.com	N	Y	Y	APP	Google Blogger (www.blogger.com)
C	MentorMob	This service allows you to arrange websites, videos, and other web content in one easy-to-navigate playlist. Playlist creators can annotate additions and order the items in whichever way they would like viewers to work through the information. Playlist viewers can navigate the list in linear fashion or jump around in the playlist order. URL: www.mentormob.com	Y	N	Y	WEB	Similar to YouTube Playlists, but it is more structured and focused
C	Prezi	Interactive presentation format that adds a dynamic element to slide presentations. Users can embed video, pictures, upload PowerPoint slides, or link content to Prezi presentations. Prezi excels at showing extended metaphor and how concepts are linked together in a visual manner. URL: www.prezi.com	Y	N	Y	APP	Museum Box (museumbox.e2bn.org) SlideShare (www.slideshare.net)
C	Animoto	Users can create customized videos from images, video, and text and include background music. Animoto has a number of different layouts, styles, and musical selections. Media can be input from a variety of different sources. URL: www.animoto.com	Y	N	Y	APP	PhotoPeach (www.photopeach.com)
C	Glogster EDU	Glogster allows users to create 'web posters' with a strong emphasis on visual elements. Users can create links in the form of pictures or buttons, and organize information and media on their Glog. Glogs can also contain interactive, colorful elements. When completed, Glogs can be embedded into wikis or other webpages. URL: edu.glogster.com	Y	N	Y	APP	Smore (www.smore.com) Easel.ly (www.easel.ly)
C	Creaza	Users create stories using a variety of multimedia. Users are guided through the creative process, including mapping out their stories, before creating their cartoons. Users can animate and narrate their stories before finishing them as one video clip that can be uploaded to YouTube or other video tools. URL: www.creazaeducation.com	Y	N	Y	APP	Digital Storyteller (www.digitalstoryteller.org) xtranormal (www.xtranormal.com)

Figure 6.3 (Continued)

"follow" feature allows you to keep up with a particular expert or commenter in a field or on a topic. You can often follow topics as well, which means that such services seek out additional information on your topic and bring it to you. In the case of a service such as Facebook the overall focus is on personal connection, but many of the services in our table were chosen because they allow teachers to capitalize on the social potential in a school-related context, one that you, the teacher, sets up and opens up to students for the research project.

All of the services identified here offer free or trial accounts. Some have upgraded memberships that offer more features for a price, but the ones we've identified all offer a fairly solid platform without additional charge. It's unlikely that you would want to incorporate ALL of these services in your classes, but you should expect to use more than one for maximum returns. Consider that when you make a PowerPoint or SmartBoard presentation, you utilize text and pictures, and possibly hyperlinks to websites and multimedia. Using online tools is no different; you might set up a wiki or a school webpage and put text, links, and web-media there. What we've tried to provide is enough information for you to consider what phase of the project you're in and then see what services might connect best for your students.

What You Should Know about Getting Started

It's advisable to let your school administrators know any time you are considering making a significant change in your teaching. It's responsible (required?) to let parents know any time you are signing their children up for an account or service, and it's absolutely necessary to work with your school IT staff if you want your equipment and connections to work as expected when you are ready to get kids online.

Many of the services that require accounts and are designed for school use also provide templates of letters that can be sent home, and you should consider taking advantage of these. Also, when a service offers both open, general accounts for the public and then separate accounts just for schools, go the extra step to get the school accounts. It's quicker to allow students to set up their own accounts, but when you take the extra time as a teacher to sign them up for school-based accounts, then you have control over their settings and more authority to set the ground rules for what can and shouldn't be posted.

Of course, all the tech tools in the world don't make student writing and thinking better automatically. In the next two chapters, we'll look at how a return to the analog devices of the paper and pen, when accompanied with some mainstays of the English classroom, can be combined with research writing in ways that stretch student thinking about their topics.

(D)RAFT into Unconventional Waters
Deepening Topic Perspectives

I first encountered RAFTing when I had the opportunity to be a fellow in a National Writing Project summer institute. I dived into the assigned reading on writing to learn and pored over pages trying to find just the right topic for my inquiry piece. I wanted to find a style of writing that would shake up traditional classroom writing assignments. Like Karin and her PassionQuest students, I wished to find a writing topic about which I could be passionate. I wanted to feel inspired. I wanted to do something different from the five-paragraph essay. Don't get me wrong . . . while the five-paragraph essay is a useful approach for beginning writers, one I taught extensively in my own classes, I believe it is meant to be a springboard to other styles of writing. Once students got a basic idea of how writing should be structured, couldn't they begin exploring a style of writing that is a marriage of structure and creativity? Or would that be too much to ask? Nanci suggested the RAFT approach, which she had been using with her content area pre-service teachers. As soon as I read the description of RAFT, I knew I had found my answer.

Being a former small town theater actor, I discovered that RAFT has an appealing blend of writing and pretending, which appeals to me because I view reading as an act of reading and pretending. RAFT is a write-to-learn writing technique that can be used across the curriculum to encourage students to role-play within the texts they are reading. RAFT gives students choices and allows them to explore a character and a situation more deeply by becoming that character.

What Is RAFTing, and Why Start the Classroom Adventure?

RAFT is an acronym that stands for role, audience, format, and topic. This method helps "students visualize a *role* for themselves, an *audience* for the writing, a text *format,* and a writing *topic* (Strong, 2006, p. 99). Part of what makes RAFT so effective is that it taps into the natural inclination of the reader to connect to a literary work: "As you become engaged in the story and emotionally attached to the characters, you splice yourself into the action. You indulge yourself in the delicious experience of living other people's lives, vicariously, through print"

(Buehl, 2004, p. 114). By turning students into characters for the assignment, students get to live the work. Live the history. Live the experience.

The RAFT strategy "engages students in a series of cognitive processes, such as reflection, analysis, and synthesis, so that they are required to transform the information from the reading material or other sources in order to complete the writing assignment" (National Writing Project & Nagin, 2006, p. 47). Students adopt a point of view that is likely not their own and speak from that specific point of view with a strong focus, while also directing their writing toward a specific audience and using a distinct format. It allows them to have a voice, a point of view that might be different from their own, and it gives them a chance to play with and to experiment with that voice, which is something that teen-agers, as Karin points out in regards to her juniors, are more than inclined to do.

Even better, this role-playing can be done in any content area, for "even . . . informational tasks invite creativity" (Strong, 2006, p. 99). This lends a relatable voice to informational texts. In a history class, a student posing as a soldier could send tweets from the battlefield. A student in a geometry class, in the role of an isosceles triangle, could write an email to his angles on the topic of their unequal relationship (Fisher & Frey, 2012, p. 145). A home economics student could write a letter from the standpoint of vitamin D to the body of a kid named Jack, informing Jack's body what vitamin D could do for it (Brozo & Simpson, 2007, p. 237). Every content area can benefit. Possibilities for cross-curricular projects abound!

Having students feel creative isn't the only advantage. Because the RAFT technique is a writing to learn activity, "it is meant to be a catalyst for further learning—an opportunity for students to recall, clarify, and question what they know and what they still wonder about" (Fisher, Brozo, Frey, & Ivey, 2007, p. 79). It is a creative application of learning, one that both students and teachers can feel great about accomplishing, because RAFT taps into the human desire to make meaningful connections.

RAFTing Is (Role-) Playing

Allowing students to take on a role and having them pretend to be someone else has its roots in the creative play of childhood. As children, nearly all of us pretended to be grownups. Some of us put on oversized clothes and "went to work" like Mommy or Daddy does, even though going to work meant going into the dining room, sitting down, opening a briefcase, and scribbling on papers. Others put on fancy clothes and pretended to be princesses. Still others dressed up like their favorite superheroes and ran down the hall, cape billowing out behind them as they ran. My daughters recently had an argument with a school friend who told them she forever gets to play Princess Peach in their Super Mario games at school because she "called it for all times" (for the record, trying to explain to your children that no one can "call" a character for all time leads to a whole lot of frustration on both sides of the conversation). Pretending happens on the playground and in the homes of children every day.

As noted by Jackson (2009), the American pragmatist John Dewey "believed that if you make learning more like *play*, as Mary Poppins did, then learning will have its own intrinsic value in 'the doing' (*Middle Works,* IX: 212)" (p. 101). Regarding RAFT writing, I believed if students could "play" with the research by taking a role within it, they would produce original, creative pieces of writing that were grounded in research, thereby creatively pairing and blending the two styles of writing.

In their work with their third-grade Language Arts and science classes, Ingrid Hekman Fournier and Leslie Dryer Edison created a role-playing activity similar to what I wanted to do with Karin's junior and senior English students. They had their students read a book by Chris Van Allsburg, the author of *Polar Express* and *Jumanji,* called *Two Bad Ants.* In it, Van Allsburg writes from the perspective of two ants that do not behave as typical ants do and decide to undertake their own adventures. This was the jumping off point for students to write their own descriptive, creative pieces from the points of view of both human and ant. They followed that activity with observational experiments detailing the behaviors of real ants about which students then wrote. Fournier and Edison noted that everyone, teachers and students alike, had a great time with the lessons. They observed, "Upon reflection, the next time we conduct these lessons, we plan to let students drive the content more" (Fournier & Edison, 2009, p. 43). This is similar to how I intended to use RAFT. With the vast difference between third graders and seniors duly noted, the potential for a change from the typical writing assignment became clear—RAFT would give students choices within choices, meaning that they would choose their research topics based on their passions and would also choose both the role that they would play within the context of their research and the form the writing would take, whether it be an email, a blog entry, or a poem.

Additionally, a study undertaken by Fen Voon reveals that role-playing as a prewriting strategy on its own helps writers write "much more" and produce "much better content" (2010, p. 547). In this experiment, students wrote argumentative essays without using prewriting strategies, additional sets of essays having used brainstorming as a prewriting strategy, and final set having used role-playing as a prewriting strategy. Eighteen percent of students met the requirements for content with no prewriting strategy, while 85 percent passed when role-playing was used (p. 547).

Role-playing works. The improvement with RAFT is that it adds a greater sense of purpose and specificity by having students select a format for writing to take, which creates the added dimension of form and audience, for the role-playing within the research to take.

RAFTing into Inquiry

I first worked with the RAFT strategy with a group of graduate-level teachers when I chose to do RAFT for my National Writing Project inquiry piece. My colleagues in the course assembled themselves into groups of three. Each group would play the role of Hamlet or Ophelia in a scene that I selected from *Hamlet*. To give them some freedom of choice, the writing format was chosen by the groups, and that choice determined the audience. For example, one group chose to write in an email format. They wrote the email from Hamlet to a friend who was studying at Wittenberg with Hamlet. Hamlet wrote to the friend about what happened that day with Ophelia at Elsinore and how Hamlet felt about it. Hamlet's reaction to the scene's events was the assigned topic for everyone. In other words, the role was Hamlet, the audience was the friend, the format was an email, and the topic was Hamlet's reaction to the events in the scene. The groups inserted themselves into the action and produced entertaining pieces of writing as a result. An unforeseen outcome was that the papers were both fun and easy to read. As a teacher, not having to sit down with a sigh because I know I have a stack of papers to slog through is fabulous. To my great happiness, Hamlet's email to his friend revealed Hamlet's conflicted indifference toward Ophelia. I found a different writing on Ophelia's diary entry to be full of angst. Most of the writing made me laugh, and all of it was enjoyable to read. That was a huge bonus. It was the opposite of Karin's Easter paper grading experience, Ham and Horror, and I was grateful and pleased it had been a success.

Core Connections

The Common Core addresses the need, beginning in grade 6, for students to "produce clear and coherent writing in which the development, organization, and style are appropriate to task, purpose, and audience" (W.6.4). Because it involves writing from a different point of view and using a specifically chosen format, RAFT writing deals quite a bit with task, purpose, and audience. This same Common Core standard wording carries through the upper-grade versions of standard 4 as well, so it is a skill that is expected of every grade level.

RAFT writings address the narrative writing elements of point of view and tone in that students should be able to establish "one or multiple point(s) of view" (W.11–12.3.a) and "create a coherent whole and build toward a particular tone and outcome" (W.11–12.3.c).

Additionally, RAFT meets the goal of having students "develop and strengthen writing as needed by planning, revising, editing, rewriting, or trying a new approach, focusing on addressing what is most significant for a specific purpose and audience" (W.11–12.5). RAFT is a step in planning and writing for the research paper, it is often a new approach for students, especially in the context of a research paper, and it certainly puts the focus on a specific purpose and audience.

Finally, using research in RAFT writing allows students to "integrate information into the text selectively to maintain the flow of ideas, avoiding plagiarism and following a standard format for citation" (W.9–10.8). It is practice for the larger paper, and builds a solid foundation for the additional writing to come.

RAFTing into Research

After Karin and I spoke about her re-imagined research paper, I couldn't help but think that RAFT, though it has not been used for research papers, could be a useful tool for students who are engaged in the research writing process. In an English class, RAFT is typically used to help students insert themselves into the action of the literature so that they can explore character and make deeper connections with the stories they read. Why couldn't the technique be utilized for research? Why couldn't students create a role for themselves within their research topics and work creatively with the nonfiction texts? We set out to see if it would work.

The day Karin's students turned in the beginnings of their research on their chosen topics, meaning that they had found sources and had completed some source documents, I had them use that research for a RAFT assignment. First, I tapped into prior learning by asking students if they'd previously written a point of view or RAFT piece. Next, we reviewed point of view by reading and discussing Shel Silverstein's "Christmas Dog," a poem written from the perspective of a dog "protecting" his home from a late-night, red-clad Christmas Eve intruder, because having students assume a point of view other than their own is an important part of the RAFT writing task. Then, I presented the RAFT format to them in a PowerPoint presentation, explained RAFT, and showed them my process in researching and working toward writing a RAFT piece. I told students that I wondered what I wonder about, just as they did for their PassionQuest research topics, so that I could find a topic I found to be meaningful. One of the things I have always wondered about is what it was like to be a pioneer on the frontier. I loved playing Oregon Trail when I was in middle school, and all of the questions I used to have came back to me. What was it like on the Oregon Trail? Could I have survived? What was a day in the life of a real pioneer like? Based on these questions and inspired by Buehl's suggestion in *Classroom Strategies for Interactive Learning,* I took the role of a frontier woman. My format was a diary entry, so my audience was myself. The topic was the hardships I was experiencing as a frontier woman in the west (Buehl, 2004, p. 115). I showed them my source document with the sources I used and the quotes and summaries I had written down. I shared the following narrative with students as a ShowMe within the PowerPoint presentation:

> *March 18, 1858*
>
> *My sweet Johnny came down with a fever today. We kept him as cool as we could with compresses on his forehead. He moaned, wailed, and cried out something fierce. We were grateful to stop for the night. When a doctor finally came back to our wagon, he took one look at him and declared that he had malaria. We made Johnny a tea ("The Prairie Pioneers") that the doctor said would help Johnny get better. Johnny winced when he drank it, but he drank it all down. What a brave boy.*
>
> *When I close my eyes at night all I can see is the image of my father running alongside the wagon as we rolled away from the house (West 35). I want to cry when I think I may never see my mother again. I may never again see her blue eyes and gentle smile, or feel the softness of her hand when she brushes my hair off my cheek. But this may be a new start for us. Once we get the land the government is giving away (Palmer 66), we'll have a new beginning. A new life. More than we had ever before. I hope it's worth it. There are many graves marked with crosses made from tree branches on this trail. We know not what may befall us. I pray Johnny survives.*

The ShowMe I created and had on the screen featured a painting of a pioneer woman surveying the land, while the audio was of me reading the text of my writing with the sound of plaintive harmonica music in the background. The ShowMe was really fun to make. I kept re-recording it to try to get my reading to end just as the harmonica music faded into silence.

After we all listened to my writing sample together, I presented students with ideas I had developed for them to write regarding their topics. I told them they could feel free to select their own roles and formats, but I wanted to provide some suggestions in case they had a tough time getting started, which was something Karin had suggested. For some classes, I created suggestions for everyone, and in others, I made just a few suggestions. Most of the students selected the ideas I provided. One student wrote a letter from the perspective of a rat living in the home of a hoarder. That example allowed her to use sensory descriptions of what the rat was seeing around it as it moved through the home looking for food. Another student researched the Great Wall of China, and he wrote from the point of view of a worker who was building the wall.

Prior to writing, students were given a rubric (Appendix C: RAFT Rubric) and knew that they had to use in-text citations in their creative writing, an activity that gave them practice with citations and held them accountable for using their previously found outside resources.

Because I believe wholeheartedly in the importance of prewriting, it is one of the categories on the rubric. I distributed a handout (Appendix D: RAFT Handout) to help them get started with note-taking. I used the writing on this handout to score the prewriting section.

Most students got full credit for their in-text citations. All of them produced original, creative pieces of writing based on a researched topic. Their writing voices really came through, and I found myself chuckling along with them as they explored their topics in a different way. It was a playful exploration, and they seemed to have fun with the assignment. Reading their papers was in no way drudgery. See their work in Figures 7.1 through 7.8.

RAFT Prewriting Handout

What is your level of RAFTing experience? Novice? Intermediate
used RAFT in classes you've taken before today?

Directions: Once you've decided on your role, audience, and format, write them along with your topic in the blocks on the left. In the blocks on the right, write down the quotes or summaries you think you may want to use in your RAFT writing. Put citation information next to the quotes and summaries so you can locate the information in your source if necessary.

	Notes:
An Interviewer Role	We have to push ourselves above + beyond. (What it takes to be a UFC fighter)
Magazine reading Audience Audience	Notes: Training is a fulltime job. (What it takes to be a UFC Fighter)
interview of Format a UFC fighter	Notes: Eating is no longer enjoyable. (What it takes to be a UFC fighter)
his training Topic and diet.	Notes: This strict diet is high in protein + includes vegetables + whole grains. (what it takes to be a UFC fighter)

Figure 7.1 Anthony plans his imaginary magazine interview with UFC fighter Jon Jones

I am going to interview A UFC fighter [illegible] Jon Jones about his training and diet.

Q. How do you train your body to get it ready?

A: Fighters have to change their bodies into machines. We have to make them as tough and as durable as humanly possible. We have to push ourselves above and beyond. Repetitive punching drills are done to toughen the skin, tendons, muscles, and connective tissues of key body parts. Body parts are intentionally pounded to make them more dense and resilient when striking. (What it takes To Be A UFC Fighter)[1]

Q: How often do UFC fighters train?

A: Well training is basically a fulltime job. (What It Takes To Be A UFC fighter)[2] I dont personally want to give out my traing information. Mark Hominick says that he trains 6 times a week, 2 times a day with Sunday off. (What It Takes To Be A UFC Fighter.)[3]

Q: Do you have to eat certain things?

A: Most deffinately! Eating is no longer an enjoyable thing for a UFC fighter. (What It Takes To Be A UFC Fighter)[4] This strict diet is high in protein and includes plenty of vegetables and whole grains. (What

It Takes To Be A UFC Fighter)[5] "Food is just fuel for the body to endure the intense sparring and endless training Sessions" (What It Takes To Be A UFC Fighter)[6]

Interviewer: Thank you for your time.
Jon Jones: No problem, anytime.

Figure 7.2 Anthony "interviews" Mr. Jones

After writing, I surveyed the students and asked if they thought the assignment made them feel more familiar with their research. Quite a few of them did. I also asked them how they felt about writing about research this way. One student liked RAFT's "'creative' twist." Another said "it was a different way of writing and it was nice to switch it up." RAFTing "made the research fun and relatable." Yet another student said, "it gave an opportunity for a light hearted writing in the middle of a daunting research paper," which I was happy to hear. One student even recognized the down-the-road application for her research paper: "I think it motivated me to find more information in areas I neglected." A student seeing future applications for her work? What could be better?

Role-playing *can and does work* for a research assignment. Students vicariously live the research, and connect to the larger concepts of their topic as they contextualize it. Look what pretending can do!

In the next chapter, we continue to help students go beyond a superficial understanding of their topic by exploring the power of comparison and metaphor and how these concepts can be used as tools for thought and composition.

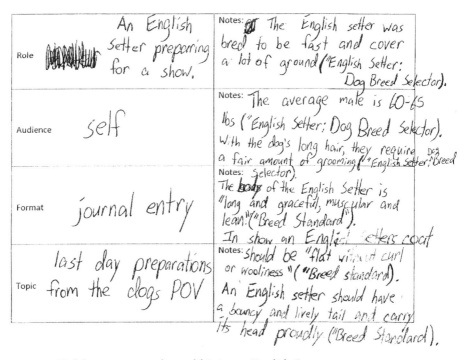

Figure 7.3 Kaleb prepares to channel his inner English Setter

Today is the last day before the annual Pa Spring Dog show. My master is really nervous. He worked me extra hard today. He made sure that I was ready to show off my speed to the judge (English Setter: Dog Breed Selector). I only got one meal today and no treats, because I'm 65 pounds and my master doesn't want to risk me being over the 60-65 pound range ("English Setter: Dog Breed Selector), that I should be in. On the plus side I got groomed three times to make sure my coat is smooth and flat, like it should be ("Breed Standard"). Although my master is nervous, I am really excited! I can't wait to show off my graceful, lean, and muscular body ("Breed Standard"). When I trot out around the ring I will hold my head high and proud and keep my tail lively ("Breed Standard"), because I am an English Setter!

Figure 7.4 Kaleb writes from the point of view of a dog

RAFT Prewriting Handout

What is your level of RAFTing experience? Novice? Intermediate? Expert? When and how have you used RAFT in classes you've taken before today? In an informal way. West civ class, English, ...

Directions: Once you've decided on your role, audience, and format, write them along with your topic in the blocks on the left. In the blocks on the right, write down the quotes or summaries you think you may want to use in your RAFT writing. Put citation information next to the quotes and summaries so you can locate the information in your source if necessary.

Figure 7.5 Lydia preps her mock television interview with a filmmaker who has first-hand knowledge of the conditions in remote areas of Afghanistan

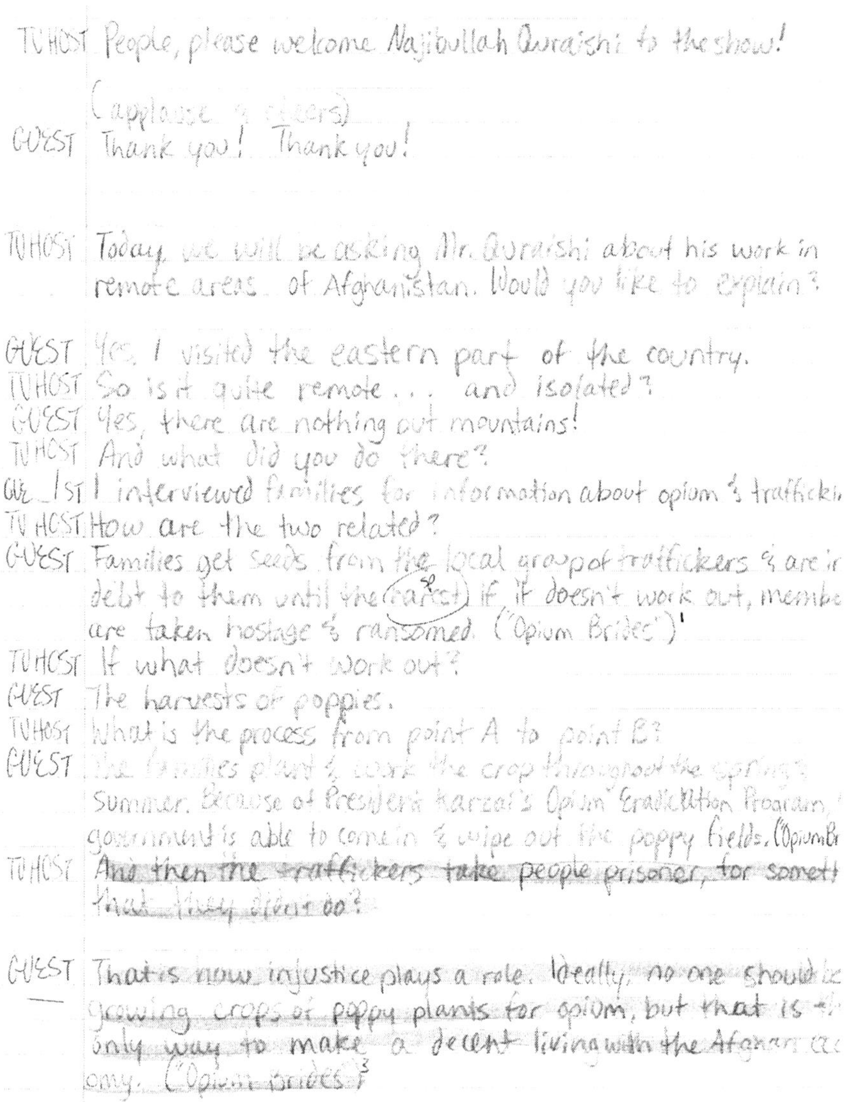

TVHOST People, please welcome Najibullah Quraishi to the show!

(applause & cheers)
GUEST Thank you! Thank you!

TVHOST Today we will be asking Mr. Quraishi about his work in remote areas of Afghanistan. Would you like to explain?

GUEST Yes. I visited the eastern part of the country.
TVHOST So is it quite remote... and isolated?
GUEST Yes, there are nothing out mountains!
TVHOST And what did you do there?
GUEST I interviewed families for information about opium & trafficking
TVHOST How are the two related?
GUEST Families get seeds from the local group of traffickers & are in debt to them until the harvest. If it doesn't work out, members are taken hostage & ransomed. ("Opium Brides")
TVHOST If what doesn't work out?
GUEST The harvests of poppies.
TVHOST What is the process from point A to point B?
GUEST The families plant & work the crop throughout the spring & summer. Because of President Karzai's Opium Eradication Program, government is able to come in & wipe out the poppy fields. (OpiumB
TVHOST And then the ~~traffickers~~ take people prisoner, for something that they didn't do?

GUEST That is how injustice plays a role. Ideally, no one should be growing crops of poppy plants for opium, but that is the only way to make a decent living with the Afghan economy. (Opium Brides)

Figure 7.6 Lydia "interviews" the documentary creator

TV HOST	What happens next?
GUEST	The families must go without the men for a little while until they raise up enough for ransom, or they must give their own children up to the traffickers. ("Opium Brides")
TV HOST	What?
GUEST	Exactly...
TV HOST	Did you say their kids? To the traffickers?
GUEST	Yes, most often the young girls are what they want.
TV HOST	That is ridiculous!
GUEST	It is a mindset. 'You can trade children like property;' the thinking has existed since ancient times. ("Opium Brides")
TV HOST	What is their fate?
GUEST	The officials I talked to wouldn't say exactly, but...
TV HOST	Abuse?
GUEST	Definitely mistreatment. It is safe to assume so, but Afghanis in power turn the other cheek when it comes to this sort of thing. The matter is very hush-hush...
TV HOST	And so you called your documentary "Opium Brides"?
GUEST	Yes, it is important to get word out.
TV HOST	Wow... people, please put your hands together for Mr. Quraishi (amid applause)
GUEST	Thanks for having me!
TV HOST	Next week, on the show, Mr. Quraishi will join the great Somaly Mam & Nicholas Kristof... See you until then!

Figure 7.6 (Continued)

Therapy Dogs offer victims of abuse unconditional love and warmth (Therapy Dogs International) (italics)

Testimonials about veterans with PTSD (prior print?) Residents learn, in the company of dogs, to overcome loneliness and fear (Therapy Dogs International) (italics)

Therapy dogs ought to be petted (TDI)

RAFT Prewriting Handout

What is your level of RAFTing experience? Novice? Intermediate? Expert? When and how have you used RAFT in classes you've taken before today?   Strong

Directions: Once you've decided on your role, audience, and format, write them along with your topic in the blocks on the left. In the blocks on the right, write down the quotes or summaries you think you may want to use in your RAFT writing. Put citation information next to the quotes and summaries so you can locate the information in your source if necessary.

Role Persuasive enthusiast compelling VA hospitals to utilize therapy dogs.	Notes: "Dogs can perceive threats from any variation in their normal environment, routine, or circumstance (arnold 31)".
Audience Directors of VA Hospitals	Notes: "Dogs and humans are both highly social, highly emotional species (arnold 169)."
Format letter	Notes: "We are just now beginning to see how dogs have the ability to heal, warm and sooth spirits of individuals with... the spirits of those who are sad and lonely (TDI).
Topic The importance of service/therapy in our society.	Notes: "Today, dogs herd for us, guide us, protect us, help police us, sniff out drugs, improve blood pressure, and provide numerous other societal benefits (arnold 31)

"That dogs have extraordinary sensory perception is undeniable, and will surely continue to discover new ways in which they use these remarkable → abilities (arnold 64)."

Figure 7.7 McKenzie plans her letter to a director of a Veterans Affairs hospital

March 20, 2013

Dear Director of Veterans Affairs Hospital,

    I have trained successful public assistance canines for ten years. Throughout my career, I have witnessed the power of canine companionship. The unbreakable bond formed between human and canine encompasses an unwavering trust (Arnold xiii).[1] Public assistance canines have proven themselves beneficial after every successful partnership I have created. I confidently believe veterans suffering physical and mental obstacles would benefit from therapeutic canine attention.

    I am aware that the majority of soldiers rehabilitating in Veterans Affairs Hospitals suffer a range of war induced disablements. Some soldiers are adjusting to physical impairments and others are battling Post Traumatic Stress Disorder (*Patriot PAWS*).[2] Soldiers leave a disheartening war to enter an unfamiliar and intimidating rehabilitation center. I firmly believe the presence of canines would soften the harsh reality soldiers must face postwar. Canines have the ability to calm and soothe agitated individuals (*Therapy Dogs International*).[3] Soldiers can feel comfortable and secure knowing a highly perceptive creature is by their side. Canines have a profound sensory skill that allows them to perceive unnatural danger (Arnold 31).[4] The presence of personal protectors reassures soldiers that they are being defended.

    In the company of canines, soldiers have the ability to break down the walls of denial that surround them. Canines help overcome the lonely feelings and fearful attitudes (Therapy *Dogs International*)[5] soldiers possess. The tickle of a puppy-kiss or the feeling of soft fur is more comforting than strange doctors' instruments. Confiding in a creature that cannot talk back is more relaxing than awkward conversations with therapists. Canines offer guidance, support, and numerous other societal benefits (Arnold 37).[6] Veterans could desperately use a new best friend of the dog variety. Please, consider utilizing therapeutic canines in your Veterans Affairs Hospital.

Sincerely,

McKenzie

Figure 7.8 McKenzie writes to stress the importance of therapy dogs for soldiers

8 Metaphors Be with You!
Organizing Connections and Building Frameworks for Comparison

"Ew. Metaphors? That's just for English class!" So typical a comment. And so untrue. Metaphors are just one figure of speech typically defined and identified in English classes and in the discussion of literature, but they are *far more than a tool for style and explication.* Simply put, we use metaphors to process the world. In *The End of Education: Redefining the Value of School,* Neil Postman writes, "We may conclude that humans live in two worlds—the world of events and things and the world of words about events and things" (1996, p. 181). Humans are hard-wired to use language to think and communicate about information, to connect events and things into our thought patterns and ways of understanding. Metaphors are perfect vehicles for this process, and the teachers and writers that recognize and harness their power will be more effective.

We use metaphors to organize how we think about reality, and, often, the more abstract a concept is, the more metaphors there are that have been created about it. Consider that your birthday passed uneventfully and your next trip to the dentist looms ahead. In the previous sentence, time was characterized first as something that was in motion and moved past you, while you remained in a fixed position, and then as a sequence of events that is laid out in front of you, with you being the object that is in motion. Consider too that even physicists can't agree on which conceptualization is accurate. Though we find metaphors in literature, we also see them in our everyday perceptions, as we "run" a computer program, bubble with laughter, horse around, and generally ride the rollercoaster of life.

Core Connections

The Common Core ELA Standards address metaphors and similes early on, setting the goal for students as early as grade five to be able to determine, interpret, and explain the meanings of metaphors in texts. By the time students have reached the eleventh and twelfth grades, their role becomes more active and complex. They are expected to create and produce language that is precise and use "techniques such as metaphor, simile, and analogy to manage the complexity of the topic; convey a knowledgeable stance in a style that responds to the discipline and context as well as to the expertise of likely readers." The shift in complexity is in keeping with the overall premise of the core framework and is also reflective of the developmental capabilities for increasingly abstract thought that are characteristic of this age span.

The New to the Known

When I work with pre-service teachers, I ask them to pick a major concept from their field, describe and contextualize it, and then create a metaphor that will help them in teaching the concept to students. My premise with this group of learners is built on nudging them away from the tendency to just cover and deliver content through lecture and notes. We focus on what it means to develop a layer of comprehension that goes beyond just the information in the text, information that is often limited to definition and related facts. Specifically, I frontload the discussion by asking the class to read and annotate Laura Pardo's article, *What Every Teacher Needs to Know about Comprehension* (2004). This article delineates the different factors that influence the meaning different readers can make from a text and sets up the idea of comprehension in accordance with schema theory. Pardo notes:

> in schema theory, individuals organize their world knowledge into categories and systems that make retrieval easier. When a key word or concept is encountered, readers are able to access this information system, pulling forth the ideas that will help them make connections with the text so they can create meaning. Schema theory involves the storage of various kinds of information in long-term memory. (p. 273)

Her article goes a long way toward establishing, for my students, that knowledge is a fluid, connected entity that is so much more complex than a sum of information. Pardo also cites Nell Duke's 2003 work with informational texts and uses Duke's metaphor for describing reading comprehension as a journey, where "readers actually move through the text, finding their way, evaluating the accuracy of the text to see if it fits their personal agenda, and finally arriving at a self-selected location" (p. 272). This article is an ideal springboard for my course in general, and for the metaphor assignment in particular. It emphasizes that while information is all around us, knowledge exists only within the human brain. When a person makes meaning of a concept, he does so by connecting it to what he already knows.

One way to help students understand a content area concept, then, is to compare it to something they already know or understand well. This is where metaphors can be used as a power tool for teaching, and I like that when I run into the "metaphors belong in English class" argument, I can actually point the class back to the Pardo article and Duke's decided nonliterary use of metaphor to describe the process of learning and understanding information.

Shifting Those Gears

Pardo and, by proxy, Duke are appropriate frames of reference for educators, but for a high school class, I knew that I would have to try a different approach to get the group to buy in to the idea that creating metaphors for their research topics was a useful effort. Peter Wayne Moe (2011) notes that he introduces the concept of metaphors as tools for writing by asking the students to help him make a list of the different words they used to describe someone who is intoxicated. He uses the resulting list, which usually consists of words like "hammered" and "plastered," to launch into a discussion on metaphors in everyday speech. Such an activity would definitely have generated some lively discussion in the high school classroom, but I believe it would have also resulted in my being uninvited to be a guest there!

In terms of the high school research project, the metaphor activity is best sequenced after the students have selected their topics and have done a considerable amount of discussion and information gathering. Ideally, it is used after the class has begun drafting their paper. I usually introduce the ideas of metaphors as tools we use to organize the world, and begin with a mixture of essential questions to frame the discussion:

- How can you use this information for wealth, power, and fame?
- Will metaphors help you get a date?
- How important are metaphors to the way we think and communicate?
- Can working with metaphors at least help you with your paper?

The metaphor activity itself starts with a short bell-ringer where the class is asked to address the following items in writing. The purpose is two-fold, to gauge where they are as a group and to warm up their brains for the activity:

Can you . . .

- Define the term "metaphor"?
- Give any examples of metaphors?
- Identify where you have heard about or encountered metaphors before now? Identify the where and when as well as you can.
- Estimate how often you use metaphors when you think/talk/write?

After collecting and reviewing the written responses, I determine the pace and sequence of activities. We move through a definition of metaphors that includes an etymological look at the root of the word. The word *metaphor* comes from a Greek word meaning to "transfer" or "carry across." Metaphors "carry" meaning from one word, image, or idea to another, and connect the two by comparison. At this point, I am treading on familiar ground, as these school students have definitely been exposed to term and definition before, even if it hasn't been internalized or stuck fast in their memories.

I move forward, providing stock examples of metaphors from canonical works, then move to examples that hit a little closer to home by listing the names of local and national sports teams. We explore the loose connections between a franchise of men in helmets chasing a rubber puck and a devastating weather phenomenon and ponder the message the people of Raleigh, North Carolina, were hoping to send when they named their NHL team the Hurricanes (or what the formerly steel-driving city of Pittsburgh was thinking when it chose the Penguins as its team name!).

We examine lists of car and truck models that conjure images of rugged wilderness (Tundra, Outback, Ram, Ranger) that have little literal connection to the assembly of wheels, steel, and internal combustion that make up the actual vehicles. Depending on your students, this activity can be accomplished by putting a list on the whiteboard, showing photographs of actual car insignias, or a taking a field trip through the school parking lot. While the concept of crafting style and polishing one's writing to finesse and delight a reader often appeals more to the female students in the room, trucks and sports tend to speak to that portion of the audience, which is often male, that can sometimes be marginalized in such discussions.

An extension or reinforcement activity that is well placed at this point is to ask students to bring in examples they have found of metaphors in their own worlds. Metaphors are used widely in advertisements, song lyrics and music (is there a country song in existence that doesn't have at least one metaphor?), as well as within news articles across topics. Awakening students to the concept at work in the real world is one way to spark the transfer of thinking and meaning-making skills beyond the classroom and to facilitate long-lasting acquisition of knowledge (Wiggins & McTighe, 1998).

At this point, I channel the work of Lakoff and Turner (1989) and begin to introduce examples that are even more pervasive in speech and thought and that require no knowledge of sports or transportation. I introduce the abstract concept of time (as mentioned earlier, this concept is particularly rich for this purpose!) and provide examples of how we use metaphors constantly in an effort to impose some sort of frame for reference or understanding on what is essentially a function of physics, so that we can relate it in some way to our human experience.

Example phrases and for group discussion are as follows:

- Ebenezer believes that time is money. You should spend your time more wisely. (Time is a resource.)
- I got to school ahead of time. Marty went back in time. (Time is a linear track that we move on.)
- Time heals all wounds. (Time as an entity capable of affecting feeling and perspective.)

As an extension activity, a simple Google search can turn up enough metaphors about time (or, for alternate topics, love, hate, birth, death, etc.) for a teacher to prepare slips of examples for each student or pairs of students to explain. (NOTE: This activity can also be a nice springboard into exploring themes!)

Once the class has a good grasp on the concept of metaphors and their uses in how we think about the world, it's time for applying this awareness to the research paper task. Often, students struggle with moving from the process of taking notes from different sources to actually writing a paper that is clearly organized, well grounded, and more than just a pile of pasted facts. The metaphor strategy can serve as the vehicle for driving a student-written paper past the wall of notes and into a cohesive ring of meaning.

Working in pairs or triads, I equip the students with two tools: a list of common items that are well-suited for serving as the "known" part of a metaphor (modified from Strong, 2006, Figure 8.1 Common items that are well-suited for serving as the "known" part of a metaphor) and a protocol that asks them to describe the topics they have researched in visual terms, as well as written (based on a cubing strategy adapted from Tompkins, 2013) and spoken words (Figure 8.2 Protocol for collaborative identification of a workable metaphor).

100 Words That Can Be Used to Build Metaphors

Adapted from Strong, W. (2006). Write for insight: Empowering content area learning, grades 6-12. Boston, MA: Pearson.

Building connections by comparing ideas can be useful for helping your reader to understand your topic.

skeleton	room	library	filter	cannon	river
valley	fruit	treadmill	money	trap	trigger
maze	water	air	computer	mirror	lens
tunnel	anvil	diamond	seed	camera	lightning
rope	armor	bait	knot	dust	parachute
root	bell	window	robot	clock	wing
battery	tide	fountain	pendulum	road	sandpaper
spice	alphabet	child	net	glue	chessboard
bag	prison	satellite	database	quilt	box
hinge	rudder	monster	landslide	pyramid	wallpaper
rainbow	index	bank	nail	onion	fence
menu	manual	match	ocean	magnet	garden
ice	mist	puzzle	mountain	sandwich	window
liquid	frame	music	pocket	plow	gear
nut	prism	parasite	pulley	treasure	tapestry
port	shovel	lamp	script	ladle	target
shadow	lock	star	bridge	rocket	field
lever	plant	balloon	well	ramp	funhouse
meteor	machine	army	umbrella	house	camp
perfume	page	oven	cauldron	flag	compass

Listen to your partner as they describe their topic, then choose at least two of the ideas concepts listed here that would make a good comparison. Write these on the back of this sheet and briefly explain your selection.

My name is_____

My partner is: _____

and their topic is: _____.

Figure 8.1 Common items that are well-suited for serving as the "known" part of a metaphor

Using his or her visual and written descriptions as a base, each student verbally describes a topic to one or more classmates. Classmates take turns listening and identifying two or more items from the list that could work as effective comparisons for the topic, and provide a written explanation substantiating the reasons for their choices. As shown in Figure 8.3 McKenzie's completed worksheet for building metaphors and Figure 8.4 McKenzie's resulting metaphor paragraph, the protocols provide enough differentiation and scaffolding to support the writers as they articulate descriptions of their topics and then stretch the information into making metaphorical connections.

Building a Metaphor

Connecting your topic to an object or idea that your reader <u>already knows about</u> can help them understand it better. Using literary devices like metaphors can also make your writing more interesting to read. Taking the time to create a connection between your topic and something else can help you to move past the copy-and-paste of note-taking and develop a much deeper understanding of your topic. It may also give you more ideas for what additional information you still need, or how to get started thinking about how to present your work. The activities below will help you get started by stretching your thinking past your source document.

GET THE PICTURE	By drawing one. Sketch a scene or situation, or draw objects that are related to your topic. Stick figures welcome!
USE YOUR WORDS	Write short phrases that explore different aspects of your topic. This part helps you think in different directions and can give you more information for your rough drafts and final written paper. You don't have to try all of them, or go in order. Read all the choices, then pick 2 or 3. 1. Describe it. (Put yourself in the middle of your topic or events surrounding your topic and write about it.) 2. Compare it. (What other things is it like? What is it different from?) 3. Associate it. (What connections between this and other things come to mind?) 4. Analyze it. (What different parts/aspects does it have? How do they work/not work together? 5. Argue against it. (Seriously or humorously, but try to put yourself in the position of someone who doesn't value your topic. What would they say to criticize it?) 6. Ground it. Where did it come from? What is the history? What will or should change?
TAKE TWO	Verbally describe your topic to your partner, using the sketch and your written answers. As you read, they should look over the list of 100 metaphor ideas and identify *two or more* possibilities for you to work with. Have them write them down. Swap roles and repeat. Possibilities (their two suggestions):
TINKER	Tinker and try out both of their suggestions in the spaces below. See if you can write a paragraph for each of their suggestions. In the paragraphs, compare your topic to the suggested idea and explain how they are the same and different.

"The greatest thing by far is to have mastered the metaphor." - Aristotle

Figure 8.2 Protocol for collaborative identification of a workable metaphor

Rubrics and grading checklists can be effective tools for communicating expectations to students about their work. Most students expect their teacher to provide rubrics for extended assignments and larger activities. However, the metaphor activity is intended to move students to begin

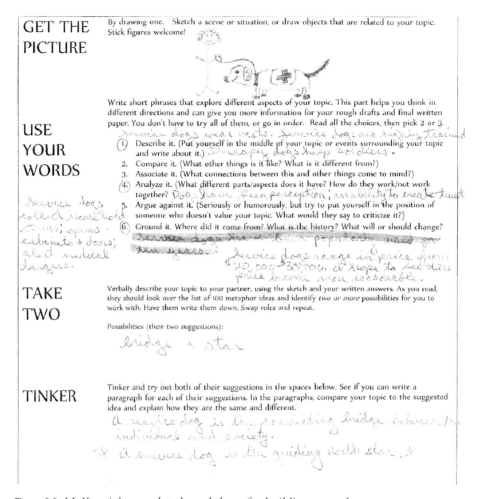

Figure 8.3 McKenzie's completed worksheet for building metaphors

The Benefits of a Service Dog

A service dog is the North Star guiding his owner through the complications of a difficult circumstance. Fixed in one loyal position and unwavering in trust, he becomes his owner's reliable comrade. Together man and man's best friend create an infinite bond deeper than the night sky. Unconditional love and support encompasses the reliable relationship. The service dog protects his owner from the realities of his disablements. He blankets the budding lonely spirits and brightens a gloomy soul. When the owner is faced with social shortcomings, his consistent comrade offers enough admiration to last a lifetime. A service dog does not weaken his owner's confidence level, because his owner is the focal point of his personal universe.

Figure 8.4 McKenzie's resulting metaphor paragraph

thinking about their topic as more than a collection of facts and dates. This approach incorporates reading, writing, listening, speaking, and use of visual representation as a means toward building higher-level thinking and making connections. As such, the following rubric (Figure 8.5 Rubric for metaphor work) was designed to offer guidance and to help students gauge their progress.

In addition to using the power of metaphors for this specific activity and for the work of the PassionQuest project in general, a post-assessment was given to the class to determine how well the activity supported their understanding of the concept of metaphors and their use in language and understanding. The questions on the assessment, which was administered six weeks after the original metaphor lesson was concluded, mirrored those on the bell-ringer/pre-assessment. The results, shown in Figure 8.6 Pre- and post-metaphor activity assessment results, revealed some respectable gains in student knowledge.

At this point in the project, students have used technology and face-to-face communication to select and narrow their topics and gather related information.

	Above and beyond: The right stuff 4	Thumbs up and smooth sailing 3	Asi-asi...effort is apparent but not productive 2	Stone wall 1 or less	Your score:
Connection	There is a fresh comparison between your topic and a seemingly unrelated item or concept, and you have made the comparison work really well in a paragraph that you developed.	You've made a strong comparison between your topic and an unrelated item or concept, and made the comparison work by providing some explanation.	A comparison has been attempted and this is clearly evident, but it doesn't really click on all four cylinders. The attempt to kick-start some movement past the facts toward a larger connection isn't working.	Huh? No connection between facts about the topic and any larger framework or other idea. Stalled and stuck.	
Style	This metaphor is written with a style that will make a reader want to keep reading.	There is evidence of style and craft in the way the metaphor is developed that will make it interesting to read.	The comparison is written out, but is still at the facts-only level, with nothing that speaks to a reader.	Not enough is written for a reader to really practice the act of reading and meaning-making	
Content	This metaphor is written with enough solid details that it will help a reader to understand your topic much better.	There a some good details compared here that will help the reader learn about your topic.	There are a few topic details here, but they are commonly known or are very general.	Little or no content is evident.	
Potential	This metaphor is so well-suited that it has the potential to be the unifying theme of your paper or presentation!	With some additional work, this comparison could become a strong part of your paper or presentation.	You tried this, but it's not strong enough to go into the paper or presentation.	No comparison, no points of information listed	
					_____16pts.
Additional activities	*Revving Up Pre-Test.* (2 points)	*Building a Metaphor.* Get the Picture (2 points)	*Building a Metaphor:* Use Your Words: 2 points	*100 Words:* Two suggestions for your partner (1 point) with clear explanations of your choices (2 points)	Total score for scaffolding and pre-writing: _____/9pts.
				Score for Metaphor Sequence:	_____/25pts.

Metaphors Be With You: A Rubric for Development and Composition (complete with mixed metaphors)

Figure 8.5 Rubric for metaphor work

Defining metaphors:	
I don't know/No answer	Decrease of 5.1%
Incorrect definition given	Decrease of 3.2%
Correct definition given	Increase of 13.0%
Example of a metaphor:	
I don't know/No answer	Decrease of 8.5%
Correct example given	Increase of 9.7%
Where and when are metaphors used?	
I don't know/No answer	Decrease of 3.4%
In and out of school	Increase of 23.1%
How often do you use them?	
I don't know/No answer	Decrease of 1.6%
Never or rarely	Decrease of 18.8%
More often than I think	Increase of 0.1%
Sometimes	Increase of 9.2%
Often	Increase of 11.1%

Figure 8.6 Pre- and post-metaphor activity assessment results

They've summarized and represented their findings in posts, written notes, and pictures, and stretched their thinking with RAFTs and metaphors. As we move into the final phases of this revamped research paper, the stage is set for draft generation, works cited, and a leap into the peril and potential of peer review.

The Nitty-Gritty
Cite, Write, Review

For many students, their first research paper is the longest single piece of writing they've ever done. It's monumental. It seems impossible. It's scary. Even though you have gotten them this far in the process, there may still be several formidable aspects in your future getting the actual paper hooked and drafted, tackling citations, and the glory of peer review and all its trappings. In this chapter, we'll explore all three, by infusing some fresh perspectives and acknowledging and taking on sticking points from the past.

With a Little Help from Our Friends

By the time our students get to the upper grades in high school, they have been asked to compose a variety of pieces of writing, to locate information for different classes and purposes, and to cite their sources. They've even had instruction on how to organize their writing clearly and to put some style into it to make it readable. Many students will stubbornly insist that this is not the case, and will do so with the most earnest of gaze and gravity of tone. Others will have retained a good deal of this instruction, but can still benefit from review and with help in getting it all to come together.

Enter into this point in our project one Matt Getz and one Levi Tinney, both pre-service English teachers who had been working with Nanci at the university. What better way to gain a fresh perspective on lessons past than having new guides put a new twist on previously trod ground?

With some advance work (including getting school-approved access to Edmodo), Matt and Levi were able to review all of the related course documents for the project to get a solid idea of where the different classes were in the overall scheme of things. They were able to read the different posts Karin's students had made earlier, where they explained their selected topics, and then they used this information to design instruction for the class.

Specifically, they prepared a lesson on how to format a Works Cited page and modeled what a strong introduction to a paper could look like. Since the class had already taken notes and recorded the source information, the citation exercises focused chiefly on technical aspects.

Because Matt and Levi were drawing on examples from papers that they were both currently actually working on, this factor lent some authenticity to the usual "you'll use this in college" admonition, and the high school students were able to see what counts as college-level writing.

They talked about hooks, background material, and how to tie the thesis to these other parts, and modeled these elements every step of the way, with the overall effect being, at times, that of advanced peer tutoring. While they were knowledgeable and professional at all times, the fact is that the students could relate to them a bit differently because of the similarity in their ages.

Matt and Levi guided students in creating outlines, refreshing their memories about outline format and the ever-popular Roman numerals. They worked collaboratively with Karin to assist students in creating outlines and preparing which "golden nuggets" of their research would best support them. From there, they taught students to create topics and topic sentences based on the assertions in their thesis statements. For some, this process was fairly simple, as their thesis statements themselves identified sub-topics. For others, some counseling led them in a direction that was reasonable, effective, and made sense to the student writer.

Finally, the students color-coded their source documents based on these topics. If a student researching leukemia, for example, started with symptoms, she'd color-code all of her information about symptoms on the source documents one color, and color that section of her outline that color, as well. After color-coding source documents, students were able to create fairly "meaty" outlines that identified not only their major topics, but precisely what bits of information they'd used to support their ideas about it when it came time to write the paper.

Because they had already completed the shorter RAFTing and metaphor pieces, the students were able to consider if these pieces could be interwoven into their papers to add more substance and cohesion for their readers.

Students reported back that the color-coding process in the outlines made the papers easier to write, as they knew where they were going at all times. Matt and Levi offered to give feedback via Edmodo after a day or two of working on rough drafts independently. They gave advice and encouragement, which those students who took advantage of the opportunity said was valuable. For additional support, Karin experimented with an iPad app called *ShowMe* to create an online presentation that used images and her own witty narration (think John Madden) to re-cap the finer points of what had been covered in class about the Works Cited pages. With this foundation in place, the drafts began developing and coming in, with many more students making substantial and ordered attempts at the drafting stage than had in previous years, and with citations, nonetheless!

With this hurdle passed, only the final challenge of peer review and revision remains. . . .

Core Connections

As we English teacher types have extolled for years, the revision process is essential to getting our best work. The Common Core State Standards support this, as well. Writing standard 5 says students need to "develop and strengthen writing as needed by planning, revising, editing, rewriting, or trying a new approach, focusing on addressing what is most significant for a specific purpose and audience." Our kids' traditional choices in revising don't typically go this far. Additionally, the College and Career Readiness Anchors for Speaking and Listening aim for students to "prepare for and participate effectively in a range of conversations and collaborations with diverse partners, building on others' ideas and expressing their own clearly and persuasively."

If You Want It, Teach It

I'm not sure who originated the phrase, "If you want it, teach it," but I myself first heard it at a training session during my first year of teaching. It's very simple, but it makes a great deal of sense. If I expect my students to be great reviewers of one another's work, then I need to show them how to do that. And yet, for many teachers, instituting peer review proves to be a waste of classroom time, with few, if any, measurable benefits. Finding the right balance and format is key.

I remember my early teaching experiences with peer review. I set up stations. Each student got another's paper and went through the stations. Station One: Look for comma errors! Station Two: Look for capitalization errors! Station Three: Look for the thesis! It seemed brilliant, but descended into a paradoxical apathetic chaos. Kids had no idea what they were supposed to be doing, and they didn't care if they did a good job. I could see Jace move to the "Comma" station, robotically flip through Sarah's paper, completely ignoring what was written there, close it, and proceed to stare, eyes a-glaze, at his own knee protruding through torn jeans for five minutes. That was the apathetic part. The chaos involved the students shifting areas frequently with thick packets of paper that were easily rolled into makeshift clubs for smacking classmates in passing.

Then I tried matching kids, followed by reading and reviewing with little explicit direction. Kids were still bored, practically drooling, and equally apathetic. Nobody had any idea what to do to peer review effectively. I was lucky if someone noted a spelling mistake. I collected rough drafts with the final drafts and, sometimes, had a hard time deciphering which was which.

As a writer myself, I couldn't understand how kids didn't see the value in peer review. Have you seen the memes out there that show a photo in which Rachel McAdams, as Regina George in the cult movie *Mean Girls,* says "Is butter a carb?" to which Paula Deen, goddess of the Southern kitchen and clogged arteries, in a second photo says, "Butter is everything, you ignorant ___"? Well, in my writer's mind, peer review was everything. I have always been confident in my writing skills, but I'm also keenly aware that I could write a paper or essay that was perfect for me, but I needed to be writing things that were appealing for my audience, too. Peer review had always helped me through that. In my college classrooms, some students would choose to review with an equally lazy friend. They were done quickly, had very little written on their papers, and discussed only last night's Tappa Kegga Dei party. I always found myself trying to find someone who was tough and who knew his or her way around an English classroom. Sometimes, I didn't even like this person. I sometimes left irritated and offended, but I knew that somewhere in the barrage of red pen marks were some terrific comments that would really tighten up the screws on that paper.

Yet, my students weren't getting this at all. Gaining feedback from others is such an important part of the writing process. How could I excite them about this step?

Do these experiences sound familiar to you? Do they match, in any way, some peer review sessions that you've tried in your classroom? Don't give up, because last year, I had one of the most miraculous days of my teaching career. I matched kids, set them forth with a checklist of "to dos," and said, "Do your best." That is the day that I witnessed "The Greatest Peer Review in Recorded Time." Young people were poring over one another's drafts as if they were brand new Harry Potter books as yet unreleased for the common man. They were reading intently and then discussing intelligently, passionately, and professionally. They asked insightful questions. They assisted with ideas and organization. They helped each other beyond measure. I was so jazzed when I went home that I even posted about it on Facebook. Only English teachers "liked" it.

This group of students was extremely conscientious and worked, typically, very hard to achieve as much as they could. How could I take their success and see that in my future students, too? That's when I remembered the Fishbowl method. While I had tried the Fishbowl approach earlier in my career while teaching students how to respond to poetry, when EMWP colleague Tina

Larson showed the potential that the Fishbowl had for peer review during one of our summer writing institutes, it made great sense.

This strategy includes putting students in the center of the room to perform or model some type of skill. Others can watch, and then we have a class discussion about how things went. Typically, students will gain both insight on what works and what some common mistakes might be. William Strong (2006) suggests giving the students in the Fishbowl various "personality" roles, like the cheerleader, the criticizer, etc., and having students on the outside reflect on how those personalities can affect the success of a peer review or other group activity. This is a terrific starting activity to teach students effective roles when working this way.

For the research project, we use the Fishbowl technique to achieve our peer review goals. First of all, you have to set those goals. And for your students, you need to set guidelines. I always talk with students about valuing one another's work. I explain that we never, ever give negative feedback that could make someone feel badly about the work they've done. I give a few examples of constructive criticism, suggestions for fixing rather than sharp statements of "wrongness": Not "Ben, you suck at commas," but "Ben, maybe you should review the comma rules."

I've been using a peer review protocol for the last few years that I like very much. I was introduced to it at our Endless Mountains Writing Project Summer Institute during a peer review activity led by Dick Heyler, our co-instructor. It focuses on what is there in terms of content and *writing*, rather than the mechanics. Be forewarned. Your students, who have been through years of understanding "peer review" to be the English teacher holiday known as the "fixing o' the grammar," will not immediately understand what is happening. Ensure them you know what you're doing and press on. Figure 9.1 shows the protocol for peer review.

Using this protocol, each student leaves with terrific, specific ideas about how to improve the writing and content. As a follow-up, I always have students sit with the same paper or papers, read, and complete a checklist (Figure 9.2) that includes other critical pieces of coherent writing, like a thesis, main ideas, MLA format, and the all-important grammar they feel they're supposed to be fixing.

Placing students in the Fishbowl to try this early protocol out can show those uncomfortable with a new peer review method just what you're striving to achieve. I've completed a Fishbowl with very intentionally chosen students I knew would give their best, and I've done the Fishbowl with students chosen at complete random. There are obvious benefits and drawbacks to both methods. Do it your way. Or, try each and see what works best for you.

I always offer extra credit to students willing to, once research papers are returned, revise them in regards to my suggestions and allow me to use them

✓ Each participant reads his or her paper aloud to the group.

✓ For each reader, you should listen to their paper.

✓ While you are listening, you are making note of the following:

1. What stands out to you? This could be a well-turned phrase, an especially engaging opening, or a fact that was new to you, for example. WRITE DOWN AT LEAST TWO.

2. What do you want to know more about? This, hopefully, is obvious. Was there something about the topic you became curious about, but didn't have your curiosity satisfied for? What questions remain with you? WRITE DOWN AT LEAST TWO.

3. What has this writer done well? WRITE DOWN AT LEAST TWO.

4. What suggestions do you have for improvement? WRITE DOWN AT LEAST TWO.

✓ Discuss together. This discussion should include each of the points you wrote down and could, and SHOULD last as long as it needs to in helping the writer improve on his or her paper.

Figure 9.1 Steps in the protocol for peer review

as future examples. They have the option to leave their names on or change them. For the Fishbowl, I select one of these papers of the past, and ask one student to play the role of the writer of that paper. Others are the listeners. They perform the protocol for the group and help those who struggle with peer review to see how valuable it can be. It's also worth noting that if you are using a service like Edmodo, you can pave the way for peer review by asking the students to post there about their projects at different stages and

---

Writer's Name: Reviewer's Name:

Checklist for Peer Review

Please place a check mark next to any question that you can confidently answer "yes" to. Leave unchecked things you think the writer should review.

First Things First:

___   1. Is the paper in MLA format (correct header, 1" margins, double-spacing, etc.)?

___   2. Is there a Works Cited page? Is it formatted correctly?

___   3. Are the in-text citations correct, according to our in-class notes?

___   4. Do you feel confident this writer has cited all the information in the paper that comes from sources?

And Then:

___   5. Does the paper have an interesting and clear title?

___   6. Does the paper open with a hook that was interesting? Be honest. Did it make you want to keep reading, or could it use a little work?

___   7. Is the thesis statement clear? Does the whole paper support it?

___   8. Does the organization make sense based on the thesis?

___   9. Do you understand everything in the paper?

___   10. Is it clear when the writer uses source material and when the words are the writer's? (Ex: Are there signal phrases when needed?)

___   11. Are there grammar issues you noticed? Did you point them out in the text?

___   12. Does the paper have unique writer's voice and interesting language?

Figure 9.2 A checklist for assisting in peer review tasks

requiring short responses from assigned partners in the class. Writers can post about their initial topic selection, about which print source they are finding to be most valuable, and which real-world sources they have identified. When students are already in the habit of reading and responding to such smaller, low-risk posts, they are frontloaded for the bigger task of peer review of full

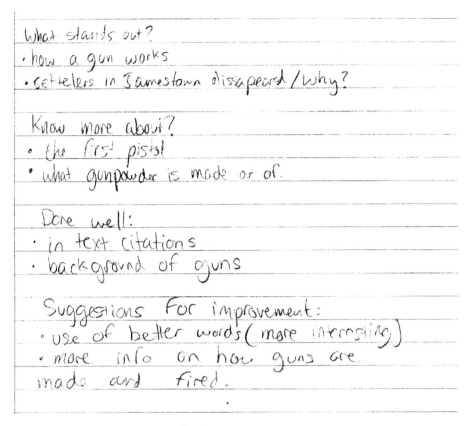

What stands out?
• how a gun works
• settelers in Jamestown disapeard / Why?

Know more about?
• the first pistol
• what gunpowder is made or of.

Done well:
• in text citations
• background of guns

Suggestions for improvement:
• use of better words (more interesting)
• more info on how guns are made and fired.

Figure 9.3 Lauren's peer review of a classmate's paper

(or sectional) drafts. An added bonus is that the drafts are digitally archived so that saving examples is a quick process. Figure 9.3 shows a completed Peer Review Protocol from reviewer Lauren for a fellow classmate/writer.

In the end, the expectations for peer review and the markers of what an effective, successful one looks like aid students in using them to their greatest advantage. Additionally, it's really a beautiful thing on peer review day to be able to look around and see that kids are doing just what you hoped they would. It's also beautiful to know it's probably because you showed them what you wanted.

Color Me Good: A Second Approach

Another way to help students envision research in a different way is through colormarking. I first heard the term "colormarking" at an AP Literature and Composition workshop one summer led by Pat Whyte. We used it there to analyze literary concepts and elements in literature. Here, we use it in a new way. The concept is simple, and requires little in the way of scaffolding, but it yields tremendous benefits for writers. Colormarking is exactly what it sounds like. Students color sections and sentences in their partners' papers, focusing on concepts that you identify. I have amassed a mammoth collection of colored pencils over the years, so I get out the tub, and we get started.

There are a variety of concepts you could focus on during research writing. Every writer struggles at some point with knowing how much of a research paper should be his or her own words, and how much should be directly quoted or paraphrased from sources. I always tell my students the paper should be primarily their words; they're using source material as support for the things they're saying. Ideally, for every fact, quote, or idea they use from a source, there should be at least one sentence before it in their own words and/or one after it in their own words explaining its value. It doesn't necessarily always happen that way when they write, though. In the heat of the research writing battle, sometimes our students are so focused on "getting it all in" that they forget that they, too, have writer's voices.

One way colormarking can work for you, then, is to ask students to take just two differently colored pencils. They should color all the words, phrases, and sentences that come from the writer in one color, and all those from source material (whether quotes, phrases, paraphrases, figures, etc.) in another color. Students may be shocked to see that the bulk of their paper is source material, and it's a good reminder to break things up a little more with their own brilliance and voice. (If your school uses a service such as Turnitin, they can submit a digital copy of their paper and the service will show, through digital colormarking and a final percentage score, similar results. While this service was originally intended to help instructors catch plagiarism, it can be effectively utilized by writers to wave a red flag BEFORE they turn the work in.)

There's really no limit to how you can colormark research papers. Maybe you've focused on transitions this year . . . use a color for that. Perhaps you're particularly encouraging style and voice in the paper . . . use a color for that. Another idea is to have students color anywhere the writer refers back to the thesis or very clearly supports it. Colormarking can focus on whatever concept(s) you think your students need to stay most aware of.

The value of colormarking is that students gain a visual understanding of how well they've achieved certain writing goals. The colors on paper can, at times, be a real smack in the face for students, a realization of what they did well, and what they may need to adjust. At times, it doesn't match with what they thought they had done, and that's why it's such a helpful technique.

Successful Peer Review? Check!

Of course, a basic way to ensure students feel confident in a peer review is to provide them with clear guidelines that inspire active work. Creating a checklist (see Figure 9.2) can give them a step-by-step method of evaluating how well another student (and they, themselves) has met certain performance standards, based on what you've taught. Checklists can be as simple or detailed as you desire, from hitting basic and general concepts like the 6+ traits of writing to individual details you've worked on together.

Peer reviewing is not just for the writer, but also for the reviewer. Seeing another's writing can be a reminder. "Oh . . . Suzie's commas are all over the place. I completely forgot to check mine, too." It can be an inspiration. "Wow . . . I like the way Jose has added so much sensory detail. I think I'll add more to my piece, too." It can be a motivator. "Mikayla's a really strong writer. If I worked a little harder, I bet I could sound more intelligent in this thing." Let your students take inspiration and motivation from one another, just as you take inspiration and motivation from them.

I've used varying degrees of checklists in my student reviews. Sometimes, it's very simple and designed to give students an equally general evaluation of what they're doing well and what they may wish to work on. Other times, I'm very specific about what I want them to accomplish. Let your objectives be your guide, and share these with your students, in terms of the rubric or checklist you are using to grade the final work, and then also with coaching/ peer reviewing expectations and modeling along the way. When we get down to the nitty-gritty of the research paper and support it just as purposefully as the earlier steps, the end result is . . . not just a hefty stack of papers, but empowered writers and reviewers.

While a hefty stack of papers IS DEFINITELY BETTER than a stack that is slim because so few students actually turned in work, the quality of those papers is a higher priority, and that students have developed real knowledge and critical and enduring skills are a few more notches in the upward spiral. This text comes to an end after the next chapter, but the work of our students doesn't have to conclude and end when the paper is printed, stapled, and added to the tower on the teacher's desk. In our last chapter, our students take on alternate and new literacies and transform their papers into formats that fit real-world audiences. In the process, they see their work extend beyond their classroom, as their voices and knowledge make an impact on and contribution to their communities.

Beyond the Paper
Impacting Wider Audiences

Congratulations. At this point, you have a stack of papers, but they aren't quite as intimidating as previous stacks of papers you've brought home to grade. These kids worked hard, and you were with them every step of the journey. No flagrant-ham-and-pie binging necessary. You can go to work on Monday and brag a little bit in the faculty room over your bagel. You've just done some really. good. teaching.

Your students are better prepared to go off to college and the work force with a solid foundation in research writing. This process has been a memorable one, in a good way; something you can really be proud of. Go now to your colleagues who have had similar research paper struggles and give them a nudge in the right direction. Share your learning . . . it's what we do!

What about your kids? With whom do you think they'll share what they've learned? Do you suspect Mom is going to place a copy of the research paper about human trafficking in a shadow box on the living room wall? Will your students sit down with their grandmothers on the front porch swing and read to them about Hitler's childhood? Boy, it would be cool if they did, but it is unlikely. In other words, since we've focused throughout the process on keeping the inquiry meaningful, why should we let the culminating work just end at the teacher's desk? If the topics were chosen because they had relevance outside of the classroom, then what are the possibilities that the students could utilize their work to become part of the larger conversation that is going on in the world about their topic? If students are going to put in that much time and work, they should be encouraged to go that extra step and share their knowledge with others outside the classroom setting. Even better, they should walk away knowing that the work they did really benefited someone. The final part of the research project is two-fold: finding an audience or forum where the work will have an impact, and reformatting it so that it is more likely to be well received there.

New Literacies? No Sweat

Lapp, Fisher, and Frey, in the May 2012 editor's message in NCTE's *Voices from the Middle,* ask, "Are you as 'literate' as your students?" They go on to define the term "new literacies" as "those ever-expanding literacies that one needs to navigate both personal and professional life" (pp. 7–9).

These are the electronic, technological tools that kids use every day to communicate and participate in their daily lives. They tweet, Facebook, and blog like nobody's business. They post pics to Instagram like pros. They Google like the dickens. They listen to podcasts and take names. They upload vids to YouTube and create mashups to beat the band. Why do they do this? "The work of new literacies is always about making connections within and across contexts and people. It is the work of sharing and communicating" (Hagood, 2012, p. 15). These forms of sharing and communicating greatly benefit students because, for better or worse, they are much more informed in so many ways about so many topics related to these literacies. New literacies can be incorporated into the classroom, and, as we have shown in Chapter Six: Are You Being Served? What Tech Tools to Use and Why You Should Bother, and throughout the project, into the research paper process, too.

Ever post something online and get a near-instantaneous response? It's exhilarating. Someone, perhaps someone thousands of miles away, received what you were communicating and reacted to it seconds after you posted it. It feels wonderful, because now, even if you are sitting with your iPad or laptop in your lap and are completely physically alone, you are connected to something bigger than yourself. You matter. What you said or did mattered at that moment. What they do in the classroom matters, of course, but if we can make it matter even more, make them more beholden to the outcome because it will be more publicly beheld than the paper itself, then why shouldn't we? We should help them make their work as meaningful as possible, and that's how new literacies can help.

On a very basic level, kids are doing word processing to write the paper and are researching online. Both of these are tools needed for the world of work in order to produce reports and fact find. Unlike turning in school papers or work reports in the past, however, new literacies gain writers near instantaneous feedback on communications they are making. "Voice mattered. Response mattered. And by response, it wasn't, 'I'll read your essay sometime in the next three weeks and get it back to you with comments and a grade.' It was the immediacy of texting or hearing from one of your numerous friends within minutes, if not seconds, after you posted" (Teng, 2012, pp. 34–35).

Students spent time "speaking to the living" while they found resources, as explained in Chapter Five. Now, it's time to take the wealth of knowledge they've gained and share it with another audience beyond the teacher who reads their papers. For some, sharing with the classroom audience is a natural fit, as their information could be beneficial to their fellow students. For others, they can take what they've learned and provide that information in some format to others outside of the school community. Imagine a student, for example, who investigated ways to easily save energy who presents this as a PowerPoint or Prezi to the principal or school board. Imagine further that they implement some of her ideas. Her work now has a powerful impact on a greater audience.

Whether they share with the class or someone else, it's important that our students share what they've done with someone who can view it in a meaningful way. Damico and Baildon (2011, p. 234) argue, "new ways are required to understand and explain the workings of an increasingly interconnected world. These new ways involve ... forging new approaches to frame and investigate problems that lead to tangible results (Polimeni, 2006), and involving a broader array of participants and stakeholders (outside of academe) in doing this work" (Hadorn et al., 2008).

For many students, the research paper itself isn't enough of a "tangible result" to get them excited and engaged. For some, it's a brochure that will be given to *real students* who are taking a mythology course for the first time. For others, it's a video about livestock showmanship that lets people who don't participate learn more, in a clever way, about the work involved. For others, it may be creating awareness in our rural school about a world problem, like endangered species or human trafficking.

Damico and Baildon note, "Transformative goals and outcomes keep us all focused on a larger picture or higher purpose of education, which is the cultivation of knowledge and skills to shape a more just and humane world. This dimension marks a move away from traditional academic goals that typically center on the acquisition or mastery of content (often cast in decontextualized and abstract ways) and toward instructional and learning goals that pivot upon specific outcomes linked directly to deeper and more empowering understandings of how to respond to pressing problems like climate change" (2011, p. 240).

Creating a product for a greater audience can be incredibly empowering, and it creates an added layer of accountability. The research paper won't simply be turned in for a grade. It'll be seen by others, by a broader audience.

Core Connections

The great part about the Common Core standards and the research paper is that the shift the core standards make toward nonfiction reading and writing means that the research paper, with its informational reading on specific topics and its many steps that require reading, analyzing, summarizing, annotating, note-taking, outlining, synthesizing, composing, revising, revising, and more revising, hit many of the standards for informational text. On page 41 of the Common Core State Standards, which details the ten items that make up the College and Career Readiness Anchor Standards for Writing, the research paper covers nine of ten, leaving out only number 3 because it regards the writing of narratives. *Nine out of ten!*

So does the idea of sharing what you've done in a different format and for a different audience. W.11–12.4 suggests that students should be able to "produce clear and coherent writing in which the development, organization, and style are appropriate to task, purpose, and audience." This alternate format changes their task, purpose, and audience, and causes students to think differently about what they're doing and about which pieces of information will best achieve that new purpose.

Standard W.11–12.5 requires students to revise and rewrite, "focusing on addressing what is most significant for a specific purpose and audience." Again, making choices based on the audience and what one hopes they will gain is a critical skill for young people. Finally, W.11–12.6 requires the use of technology to "produce, publish, and update individual or shared writing products in response to ongoing feedback, including new arguments or information." Remember Chapter Five: Speak to the Living: Real Sources, Real Audiences? Students were able to gain perspectives from others, and in some cases, overt response to their own survey questions. This final piece, especially when the audience and the "living source" match up, gives an opportunity to use that primary research to make plans for presentation.

Finding the Audience

Your students will need to spend some time considering what person or group of people might enjoy or benefit the most from the information they have found. Encourage them to find the best audience they feel they can, offering suggestions when appropriate, even if that audience doesn't extend outside your classroom walls.

Offering a few examples of audiences and products that work can be great inspiration. For example, one student had researched trapping. His living source was our biology teacher, who happened to devote his out-of-school time to hunting, trapping, and all things outdoors. This teacher, Jim Mucci, had been supportive of our project along the way, including sharing with us that he donated time to several outdoor organizations and events. This student ended up creating a brochure that Mr. Mucci could make available at the Youth Field Day he assisted with at a local state park, something tangible the kids who attended the event could have as a future reference.

Another student studied the history of guns, finding some truly fascinating weaponry from ages past. His class had a number of students who hunted, and while we were researching, it was common to hear some "oohs" and "aahs" when he stumbled on a particularly unique piece of history in the chain. Down the road from our rural school is a sporting goods store. I suggested he create a visual timeline and allow the store to display it. In the end, both he and the student studying trapping shared information with classmates, but they were duly enthralled with the information they shared. Time constraints likely got the better of the timeline plan, so moving forward, I'll add more time to the deadline on this part of the process and perhaps offer incentives for going beyond our classroom with the information.

Students should also return to their "living" sources. They may make terrific audiences for this information. Remember my student who investigated Nike, Inc.? His living source was a local shoe storeowner, and in the end, he created a PowerPoint that gave both facts about the company and the storeowner's perspectives about consumers' shoe/sneaker choices. She'd probably both enjoy and benefit from hearing what other information he found about a company she so frequently deals with.

In the past, I've had several students research the history of their favorite sports teams. One, in particular, I can remember being an avid Yankee fan. Often, this kind of thing is generational. For this project, she could have interviewed her father or grandfather about what they think are the Yanks' greatest moments and created a Prezi that displays what from her resources and her interview are the ten most important things that happened. Her audience could simply be her dad or grandfather, and would lend itself to a terrific conversation moving forward.

Finally, I've seen students research different weight loss programs. She could interview people who have tried the ones she's comparing, and share this in a poster format with the school nurse, who at times may counsel students looking to lose weight and get healthy.

In this first shot at expanding audience, few students stepped out of the school walls. Classmates and members of the school community who benefitted from the research gave positive feedback to me and to one another, so it was a success on a different level for sure. As I approach this task again in the future, I plan to give students more time to find their very best audience, and more time to execute. The planning for audience and format could happen concurrently with writing the paper, as opposed to starting after the paper is complete. Additionally, I'd suggest offering an incentive for those who take the information "to the people" outside their classroom.

A Brand New Format

After your students have identified audiences for this information, it's time to think about the best way to present their information. Most of our students are fairly adept at some terrific means of presenting via technology, and there are others, too. The students will ask, and maybe the question is in your head, too: "Do I have to cite my information?" The answer is a resounding "yes!" This is not only an opportunity to engage in authentic work, but to see that plagiarism is plagiarism, whether it's typed on a page or it's a picture you've picked up through Google Images.

Following are some common presentation formats that may help students to create some exciting new formats for their information. The technology tools are explained in more detail in Chapter Six, but here's a reminder of the many ways your students can share information:

- **Prezi**—This tool does PowerPoint one better, creating a truly visually exciting presentation of information with flying graphics and content. Students are becoming accustomed to using it, and for a lot of out-of-school audiences especially, a Prezi can be incredibly impressive and engaging to watch.

- **PowerPoint**—It's a classic for a reason. It allows students to summarize the most important bits of their information, add music and video, and set up a slideshow to share without speaking, if they desire. If they're sharing with an audience to whom they need to share digitally, the message can be shared without the need for verbal explanation, too.

- **Movie**—Our students LOVE to make movies. I've had several create powerful MovieMaker or iMovie projects using images and words and music coming together in a very meaningful way.

- **Brochure**—For some of our students, sharing the information with others as a take-home makes the most sense. There are many simple programs to do this at students' fingertips. Most school computers come standard with either Microsoft Office, which could include Publisher, or Apple's Pages program, which also has a brochure option.

- **Poster**—Considering the surveys many of our students did, it was clear that our school community didn't have a lot of information about some topics. A poster to hang in the cafeteria or hallway can be a means of sharing more with a larger audience.

- **Timeline**—Many of our students use history as a topic or a famous person's biography, or the progression of a company or sport. The timeline is a new way of presenting information that is visually appealing and can utilize images, quotes, facts, and more in a different way.

- **Blog**—It's easy and free to set up a blog these days, and typically, people find it. Students can post blog entries about their topics, using their information to support the ideas they're sharing with the world.

Figure 10.1 shows some of the alternate formats and potential audiences students have chosen. Figure 10.2 shows Whitney's brochure about shark

Topic	Audience	Format
Muhammad Ali	Classmates	Timeline of the significant moments in his life, driven by a survey showing people knew little of his background in our school.
Canine therapy	Local senior care facility	PowerPoint about the benefits of canine therapy
Livestock showmanship	Classmates and 4-H group	PowerPoint and movie "So God Made a Show Kid."
Trapping	Young people interested in the outdoors at Youth Field Day	Brochure of basics
Archery	Classmates	Video of her and her dad showing the critical elements of two types of bows
Forensic Science	Older high school students	Brochure about what to study in high school and which schools in our general area have strong programs
Adolf Hitler	History teachers	PowerPoint with less common information about Hitler's background
Greek Mythology	Students enrolled in next year's mythology course	Brochure of basic things everyone should know about mythology
World War I	Classmates	Prezi of key causes leading to the war
Shark attacks	Friends, family members	Brochure on how to avoid being attacked at the beach

Figure 10.1 This table shows some of the alternate formats and potential audiences students could have chosen

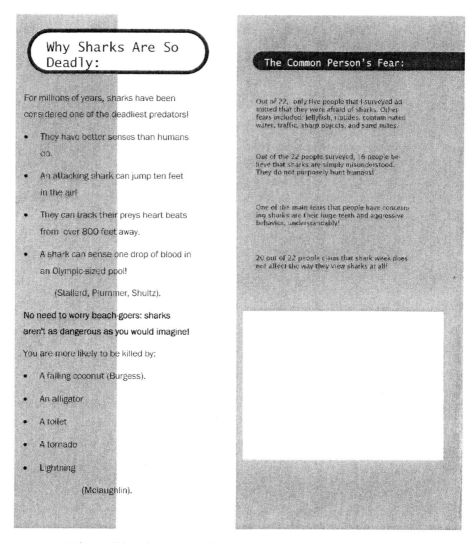

Why Sharks Are So Deadly:

For millions of years, sharks have been considered one of the deadliest predators!

- They have better senses than humans do.

- An attacking shark can jump ten feet in the air!

- They can track their preys heart beats from over 800 feet away.

- A shark can sense one drop of blood in an Olympic-sized pool!

    (Stallard, Plummer, Shultz).

No need to worry beach-goers: sharks aren't as dangerous as you would imagine!

You are more likely to be killed by:

- A falling coconut (Burgess).

- An alligator

- A toilet

- A tornado

- Lightning

    (Mclaughlin).

The Common Person's Fear:

Out of 22, only five people that I surveyed admitted that they were afraid of sharks. Other fears included: jellyfish, riptides, contaminated water, traffic, sharp objects, and sand mites.

Out of the 22 people surveyed, 16 people believe that sharks are simply misunderstood. They do not purposely hunt humans!

One of the main fears that people have concerning sharks are their huge teeth and aggressive behavior, understandably!

20 out of 22 people claim that shark week does not affect the way they view sharks at all!

Figure 10.2 Whitney's brochure about shark attacks

attacks. Figure 10.3 shows a brochure Grace made after researching forensic science as a career. She plans to place copies in the guidance office for use when students tell our guidance counselor they are interested in the field.

In Conclusion . . .

Ultimately, we three English teachers believe we have provided you, our readers, with tools that will aid you in re-designing how you approach and implement the research paper in a new, updated way. Announcing a research paper as the next assignment doesn't have to inspire loathing. Providing activities that help

Does the mystery of crimes intrigue you?

If so, a career in forensic science may be what you're looking for!

Works Cited

Woolcock. John. "The Forensics of C.S.I." Indiana University of Pennsylvania. 14 December 2012. Web. 2 May2013

" Forensic Science: Eberly College of Science." Penn State University. 4 July 2011. Web. 2 May 2013.

Math Picture- Sanchez, Kris. "Math Does Really Hurt." Uber Facts. 3 June 2012. Web. 2 May 2013.

Crime Scene Picture- "Mystery and Crime Fiction Month." 4 January 2009. Web. 2 May 2013.

Science Picture-Schmidt, Charles. "FAU" Florida Atlanta University. 3 March 2006. Web. 2 May 2013.

Stick Pictures- Willingham, Daniel. "Education for the 21ˢᵗ century." Britannica Encyclopedia Blog. 1 December 2008. Web. 2 May 2013

Nute, Dale. "Advice about a career in forensic science." Florida State University. 7 August 2012. Web. 24 March 2013.

Penn State Picture- "Penn Live." The Patriot News. 3 August 2008. Web. 2 May 2013

IUP Picture-"Indiana University of Pennsylvania." Colleges. U.S. News. 9 February 2011. Web. 2 May 2013.

Hamilton, Beverlea. Personal Interview. 30 April 2013.

Introduction

Deciding what area of forensic science that you would like to study can be very difficult (Nute)! There are so many career choices!

The career you choose to pursue should be based on what you can handle (Nute). Also, it should depend on how long you are willing to go to school.

For the most basic job in forensic science you need a bachelor's degree. With this degree you can do mostly lab work such as working with DNA. The higher the degree you get the better the careers you can choose from (Hamilton).

What classes should you take in high school?

Our school offers many classes that will help you learn about forensic science (Hamilton). Taking math and science courses is the most beneficial way to prepare you to go to college for forensics (Hamilton). However, health related classes also help you a lot.

Some important science classes that would be beneficial are Physics, Chemistry, and Anatomy& Physiology (Hamilton). It is also really important that you take as many math classes you can.

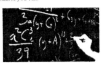

Colleges Near Us
Two colleges near us, that are known for having a good forensic program, are Penn State and IUP (Hamilton). You can visit the websites of these colleges for any questions or information, not answered or not found in this brochure!

IUP

IUP has a great forensic program. There are many interesting classes that you can take there that have to do with forensic science. For example, there is classes for computer forensics and forensic chemistry. With computer forensics you learn how forensic people use computers to solve crime and how computers are used by criminals. In forensic chemistry there are a variety of topics you could learn about. Some of these topics are the forensic chemistry of drugs, arson, poisons, hair, fibers, glass and fingerprints (Woolcock). Go to this website for information about the college.
http://www.iup.edu/default.aspx

Penn State

Penn States has a forensic program for undergrads as well as a graduates (Forensic Science: Eberly College of Science). Students are given a great foundation on biological and physical sciences. Students in the undergrad program are also introduced to topics relating to forensic science, such as forensic chemistry, anthropology, biology, and certain social sciences. In the graduate program, students have more opportunities with hands on experience with criminal investigations and lab work. State of the art crime scene training facilities and crime labs are used. For any further information go to this website.
http://forensics.psu.edu/program

Penn State

IUP

Figure 10.3 Grace's brochure made after researching forensic science as a career. She hoped to leave copies in the guidance office for our counselor to use with students interested in studying the field in the future

students narrow down their interests and passions and then use those discoveries in their research papers not only improves the process for the students, but it also improves the product, both the paper itself and the presentation, no matter what form the presentation takes. The more personally meaningful the topic, the more personally relevant the learning, and that is what moves short-term information into long-term memory.

All in all, 92.6 percent of students involved in the research project completed both the final paper and the final project. Forty-two percent of those students turning in a paper earned a 90 percent or better.

From the Student Perspective

Shanelle, a junior in one of Karin's classes, wrote this at the close of the project:

> When we first started I was terrified. I thought there was so much to do and I didn't think I was going to have enough time. In the end it was actually fun and I learned so much about my topic. . . . Asking all the questions about what we wanted to learn about really helped me to decide what I wanted to do my paper on. . . . In the end, I didn't mind the research paper, I actually liked it.

Taking this approach also allowed us greater freedom of topic. Instead of using the familiar-but-limiting list of topics, a staple in many English classrooms, students imagined better, more personally relevant topics. They learned how to evaluate sources for credibility so that they not only are more adept at finding research that works, but also at finding information in their everyday lives that is legitimate. We've all seen the recent commercial with the young lady who thinks everything on the Internet is true and who, at the end of the commercial meets up with her date, the "French model." Learning to evaluate sources can help ensure our students grow up with a little more "What's true?" savvy, whether they're navigating research in college or trying to find more information on a local event.

Students also learned ways to gather and organize their credible information that they hadn't seen before. Student Debra wrote "After I chose my topic, I began to research, and I must say I *love* source documents! The source documents helped me stay organized and keep my thoughts clear. I liked how I could number them and keep them in order."

Technology, including new literacies, is engrained in the new research project, too. It's not the same animal it was when note cards and card catalogs were the tools of the day. Texting and Facebooking and tweeting are commonplace among our audience, the students. We now live in a world where a person can make a living being a blogger. A blogger! There is another means of being a writer without being officially published by a publishing company! (Though having a publisher certainly has its benefits. [Ahem! We're looking at you, Eye On Education.] Kids engage in the act of writing more than ever before. They communicate in writing constantly, so why not build on that as an instructional strength?)

Many schools still have slow Internet access tied to antiquated computer and operating systems. It takes a while for money to catch up to technology. Regardless, all is not lost. Many of our techniques do not require computers, though some of the really interesting newer (or new as of our print date) stuff, like Edmodo and Diigo, does require Internet access. The students we taught had access during school on lab days, and most had access from home, which seems par for the course for student Internet access in general. No need for your district to have the extras for this reinvention to work.

Our new project also encouraged students to "speak to the living" to gather new perspectives and new insights, and, thus, new territory that they weren't able to gain from the printed word of the sources they found online and in our library. Student Kaleb wrote about the "speak to the living" component, "It forced me to do something I wouldn't usually do. I enjoyed getting out of my comfort zone and plan on using interviews as sources in the future."

Both RAFT and metaphor brought traditional classroom staples to the forefront and reimagined them in the context of the research paper. By doing this, students looked at informational writing differently, broadening their perspectives beyond fact-finding and plagiarism-avoiding.

We've also tried to find and demonstrate ways to makes some of the "nitty-gritty" a little more enjoyable, like the former drudgery of tasks like outlines. By creating a visually exciting means of accomplishing this task, we aimed to help students "see" the work they were doing in a way they could more easily understand.

Trying out the peer editing Fishbowl brought some liveliness to this "school." Yeah, we said it. Students engaged with one another in a way that they may not have before seeing it in action. They don't always do what we want them to do because they don't always know what we mean when we tell them what to do. The Fishbowl is a way to bring clarity and effectiveness to what for some is a really confusing and boring part of this process.

Finally, creating an alternate format is a critical piece of bringing engagement to students' research experience. It's no longer just for a grade or just for the teacher to read. It's for real people. Paired with a topic they love and learning they've gained, some are simply itching to share what they discovered.

Isn't that what teaching is all about? The final project ensured that the hard work they did would go on. Some will see it when a younger brother or sister brings home in a few years the brochure they made for the mythology teacher to use to get the ball rolling. Others will get feedback from larger audiences, possibly extending their personal network into connections that will serve them after graduation. You'll also see it in the animated conversations you and students share as they tell you about the new things they're discovering in the process.

And that's the joy of this too, isn't it? When you have a roomful of kids who are excited about the things they're learning, and they're sharing them with you in conversation, and you can see the passion in their eyes and hear it in their voices when they're sharing with the class what they've learned, when they can bring it full circle and connect their academic skills with the real world . . . you've done your job and done it well.

Appendices

Sample Research Project Requirements and Timeline

Paper Requirements:
- Typed, 12 point Times New Roman or Arial font
- Double-spaced, 1" margins all around
- MLA Citation and Format
- At least 10 qualified sources
- 5–6 pages in length

A Note on the Timeline

Some assignments will require significant class time for students to work with access to you and, in some cases, your library staff. For others, you'll have students working on their own time. This is how I manage to complete a lengthy task and all the other topics in our curricula, too. Students likely won't need class time and your full attention while working on all of these tasks. This is a good time to move forward with other subject matter in your course.

For example, if they've been doing thesis statements for years, or you've previously worked with them in your course, you may feel comfortable assigning that without class time to work. Use your discretion about when you'll be using your class time for research tasks and when you'll be having students work outside of class while you work with different material.

This timeline is based on daily, 40-minute class periods.

Assignment	Points	Due Date
Final Topic, Research Questions, and Parent Signature	25	Six weeks prior to final due date
Prior to turning in the above assignments, students will have had ample time to consider and investigate potential topics. See topic selection ideas in Chapter Two, and consider how to develop inquiry and questions about topics in Chapter Three!		
One Completed Source Document	25	One Week Later
Following topic selection, students should have lessons on finding and evaluating sources and completing source documents. We also spend time together in the library and on computers, so that they have access to the librarian and teacher as they work. Chapter Four discusses the Source Document.		
50+ Facts on Source Documents—(on any number of source docs; All ten docs not necessary!)	25	Three days Later
I keep students in the library during class until this assignment is due, as some don't have access to sources at home.		
Ten Source Documents Completed	25	Three days later
While students complete source documents on their own time, we prepare for the RAFT activity below. See Chapter Seven!		
RAFT Activity	25	Two days later
We work together on the prewriting and drafting for RAFT, and then students are on their own to complete the final product.		
Metaphor Activity	25	Two days later
Similar to the RAFT, we work together on the Metaphor lesson, and the prewriting work will require a partner, so we do that in class. Again, students are sent to do their final drafts on their own. Chapter Eight discusses the metaphor writing activity!		
Works Cited Page	25	Two days later

Assignment	Points	Due Date
Students will already have source citations completed and on their Source Documents (and sometimes in a service like NoodleTools or word processing citation feature), so a one-day lesson on how to format a Works Cited page is typically enough. Some students' computer skills are limited, and when this is the case, we start this in class, and students are assigned to finish outside of class.		
Thesis Paragraph	25	Two days later
Depending on students' familiarity/skill with thesis statements, you may spend a day reviewing or feel comfortable setting them loose. This assignment in my class is not solely the thesis sentence, but the entire introductory paragraph, including a hook to grab attention, any background information necessary for the common reader, and the thesis. Scaffold as necessary!		
Outline	25	Three days later
Chapter Nine discusses how to assist students in organizing their information. A lesson on this process and some guided work is helpful.		
Rough Draft (Entire Paper)	25	One week later
We walk through guided practice with how to create a complete paper from the outline. After that, I ask students to work on this on their own, outside of class, time. A day before this is due, it's a good idea to try your Peer Review Fishbowl. We peer review (See Chapter Nine) on the day the rough draft is due. I do not collect these papers, but rather, allow students to do their great work at review, and I walk around and look at each draft to ensure they're of appropriate length, they've used in-text citations, and I've addressed any issues I notice.		
Final Draft (Entire Paper)	75	One week later, following peer review
Students are on their own to take their peer reviewed drafts and revise them to delicious research paper perfection!		
Multimedia Presentation	75	One week later
See Chapter Ten for ideas about how students could share their work. I typically give them plenty of class time to work on this task.		
Total Point Value of Paper	**400**	

Sample Research Paper Rubric

5 = Excellent   4 = Good   3 = OK   2 = Fair   1 = Poor

MLA – Are your sources and ideas listed in appropriate
MLA citation?   _____

Are all your researched elements cited?   _____
Please note . . . plagiarism may apply otherwise, including a failing grade!

Are your in-text citations correct?   _____

Is the paper in MLA format on all levels (headers,
margins, etc.)?   _____

Focus – Is your thesis statement clear and specific?   _____

Does your thesis present an argument or stance?   _____

Content – Does your paper cover enough of the topic
to seem complete?   _____

Does your paper's content support your thesis
statement throughout?   _____

Is your paper of appropriate length?   _____

Organization – Does your paper flow from point to point
with logical order?   _____

Do you have a compelling introduction
and conclusion?   _____

Conventions – Do you demonstrate a command of spelling?   _____

Do you demonstrate a command of grammar?   _____

Sources – Have you selected the most appropriate sources
for your topic?   _____

Style – Does your paper have voice and interesting
language?   _____

Total Grade _____ / 75

Comments:

RAFT Rubric

RAFTing into Research Rubric

	5	3	1
Prewriting	Prewriting includes at least ten lines of drafting using prewriting strategies.	Prewriting includes at least five lines of drafting using prewriting strategies.	Prewriting includes four or fewer lines of drafting using prewriting strategies.
Point of View	Role chosen is appropriate for the topic, and writing does not stray from chosen point of view. Point of view is clear, and character is fully developed.	Role chosen is appropriate for the topic, and writing mostly does not stray from chosen point of view. Character is mostly developed.	Role chosen is not appropriate for the topic and/or writing strays from point of view. Character is not developed.
Format	Format chosen is appropriate for the topic. Writing does not stray at all from format. Understanding of audience and sense of purpose is clear.	Format chosen is appropriate for topic. Writing mostly does not stray from format. Sense of purpose is unclear.	Format chosen is not appropriate for topic and/or writing strays from format. Sense of purpose is unclear.
Citations	Final copy includes at least five or more in-text citations.	Final copy includes three or four in-text citations.	Final copy includes two or fewer in-text citations.
Conventions	Contains no or few errors that do not confuse the meaning of the piece. Writing flows well.	Contains several errors that do not confuse the meaning of the piece.	Contains a number of errors that may or may not confuse the meaning of the piece.

RAFT Handout

RAFT Prewriting Handout

What is your level of RAFTing experience? Novice? Intermediate? Expert? When and how have you used RAFT in classes you've taken before today?

Directions: Once you've decided on your role, audience. and format. write them along with your topic in the blocks on the left. In the blocks on the right, write down the quotes or summaries you think you may want to use in your RAFT writing. Put citation information next to the quotes and summaries so you can locate the information in your source if necessary.

	Notes:
Role	
Audience	Notes:
Format	Notes:
Topic	Notes:

References

Alvey, T. L., Phillips, N. C., Bigelow, E. C., Smith, B. E., Pfaff, E., Colt, W., . . . Ma, J. Y. (2011). From I-Search to iSearch 2.0. *English Teaching: Practice and Critique, 10*(4), 139–148.

American Association of School Librarians. (2007). Standards for the 21st-century learner. American Library Association. Available: www.ala.org/aasl/standards. Free downloadable booklet describing Skills, Dispositions in Action, Responsibilities, and Self-Assessment Strategies for 21st century learning.

Bean, T. W., Moore, D. W., Birdyshaw, D., & Rycik, J. A. (1999). Adolescent literacy: A position statement. International Reading Association. Available: www.reading.org/Libraries/Position_Statements_and_Resolutions/ps1036_adolescent.sflb.ashx

Beaton, A. M. (2010). Student choice in writing: Reflections on one teacher's inner struggle to relinquish control. *Schools: Studies in Education, 7*(1), 111–121.

Bechar-Israeli, H. (1998). From <Bonehead> to <cLoNehEAd>: Nicknames, play, and identity on Internet Relay Chat [Electronic Version]. *Journal of Computer Mediated Communication, 1*(2). Available: http://jcmc.indiana.edu/vol1/issue2/bechar.htm

Bellanca J., & Brandt, R. (2010). *21st-century skills: Rethinking how students learn.* Bloomington, IN: Solution Tree Press.

Benjamin, A., & Hugelmeyer, M. (2013). *Big skills for the Common Core.* Larchmont, NY: Eye On Education, Inc.

Blanton, W. E., & Wood, K. D. (2009). The case for improving adolescent literacy instruction. In W. E. Blanton & K. D. Wood (Eds.), *Literacy instruction for adolescents: Research-based practices.* New York, NY: The Guilford Press.

Broskoske, S. L. (2007). Prove your case: A new approach to teaching research papers. *College Teaching, 55*(1), 31–32.

Brozo, W. G., & Simpson, M. L. (2007). *Content literacy for today's adolescents: Honoring diversity and building competence* (5th ed.). Upper Saddle River, NJ: Pearson.

Buehl, D. (2004). *Classroom strategies for interactive learning* (2nd ed.). Newark, DE: International Reading Association.

College Board. (2004). *Writing and school reform and the neglected "r"—the need for a writing revolution.* National Commission on Writing. New York, NY: College Entrance Examination Board.

Common Core State Standards Initiative. (2010). Available: www.corestandards.org

Damico, J., & Baildon, M. (2011). Content literacy for the 21st-century: Excavation, elevation, and relational cosmopolitanism in the classroom. *Journal of Adolescent & Adult Literacy, 55*(3), 232–243.

DeSena, L. H. (2007). *Preventing plagiarism: Tips and techniques.* Urbana, IL: National Council of Teachers of English.

Duke, N. (2003). *Comprehension instruction for informational text.* Presentation at the annual meeting of the Michigan Reading Association, Grand Rapids, MI. In Pardo, L. S. (2004). What every teacher needs to know about comprehension. *Reading Teacher, 58*(3), 272–280.

Federal Education Policy and the States, 1945–2009: A Brief Synopsis States' Impact on Federal Education Policy Project. (January 2006, revised November 2009). New York State Archives, Albany. Available: www.sifepp.nysed.gov/edpolicy/research/index.shtml

Fen Voon, H. (2010). The use of brainstorming and role-playing as a pre-writing strategy. *The International Journal of Learning, 17*(3), 537–558.

Fisher, D., Brozo, W. G., Frey, N., & Ivey, G. (2007). *50 content area strategies for adolescent literacy.* Upper Saddle River, NJ: Merrill/Prentice Hall.

Fisher, D., Brozo, W. G., Frey, N., & Ivey, G. (2011). *50 instructional routines to develop content literacy* (2nd ed.). Boston, MA: Pearson.

Fisher, D., & Frey, N. (2012). *Improving adolescent literacy: Content area strategies at work* (3rd ed.). Boston, MA: Pearson.

Fletcher, R. (1999). *Live writing: breathing life into your words.* New York, NY: HarperCollins.

Fournier, I. H., & Edison, L. D. (2009, Summer). Linking science and writing with *Two Bad Ants. Science & Children, 46*(9), 41–43.

Freire, P., & Macedo, D. (1987). *Literacy: Reading the word and the world.* Westport, CT: Bergin & Garvey.

Frisch, K., & McLeod, S. (2007–2011). *Shift happens.* Available: http://shifthappens.wikispaces.com/

Graham, S., & Perin, D. (2007). *Writing next: Effective strategies to improve writing of adolescents in middle and high schools: A report to Carnegie Corporation of New York.* Washington, DC: Alliance for Excellent Education.

Hadorn, G. H., Hoffmann-Riem, H., Biber-Klemm, S., Grossenbacher-Mansuy, W., Joye, D., Pohl, C., . . . Zemp, E. (Eds.).(2008). *Handbook of transdisciplinary research*. Bern, Switzerland: Swiss Academies of Arts and Sciences/Springer, as cited in Damico, J., & Baildon, M. (2011). Content literacy for the 21st-century: Excavation, elevation, and relational cosmopolitanism in the classroom. *Journal of Adolescent & Adult Literacy, 55*(3), 232–243.

Hagood, M. C. (2012, Summer). Risks, rewards, and responsibilities of using new literacies in middle grades. *Voices from the Middle, 19*(4), 10–16.

Harvey, S. (1998). Nonfiction matters: Reading, writing, and research in grades 3–8. York, ME: Stenhouse.

Head, A., & Eisenberg, M. (2009, February 4). *What today's college students say about conducting research in the digital age.* Available: Project Information Literacy website: http://projectinfolit.org

Jackson, B. (2009). Role-playing in comp—Fake it 'til you make it. *Writing on the Edge, 20*(1), 99–107.

Jones, R. (2012). The Luddites: At war with the future. *History Today, 62*(5). Available: www.historytoday.com/richard-jones/luddites-war-future

Lakoff, G., & Turner, M. (1989). *More than cool reason: A field guide to poetic metaphor.* Chicago, IL: University of Chicago Press.

Lapp, D., Fisher, D., and Frey, N. (2012). Editors' message: Are you as "literate" as your students? *Voices from the Middle, 19*(4), 7–9.

Leu, D. J., Jr., Kinzer, C. K., Coiro, J., & Cammack, D. (2004). Toward a theory of new literacies emerging from the Internet and other ICT. In R. B. Ruddell & N. Unrau (Eds.), *Theoretical models and processes of reading* (5th ed.) (1568–1611). Newark, DE: International Reading Association.

Luke, A., & Woods, A. (2009). Critical literacy in schools: A primer. *Voices From the Middle, 17*(2), 9–18, as cited in Damico, J., & Baildon, M. (2011). Content literacy for the 21st-century: Excavation, elevation, and relational cosmopolitanism in the classroom. *Journal of Adolescent & Adult Literacy, 55*(3), 232–243.

Moe, P. W. (2011). Rethinking metaphor: Figurative language and first-year composition. *Teaching English in the Two-Year College, 38*(3), 282–290.

Nagin, C. (2006). *Because writing matters: Improving student writing in our schools.* San Francisco, CA: Jossey-Bass.

National Commission on Writing in America's Schools and Colleges. (2003). *The neglected R: The need for a writing revolution.* New York, NY: College Board.

National Commission on Writing in America's Schools and Colleges. (2004). Writing: A ticket to work . . . or a ticket out: A survey of business leaders. New York, NY: College Board.

Pardo, L. S. (2004). What every teacher needs to know about comprehension. *Reading Teacher, 58*(3), 272–280.

Pew Research Center's Internet & American Life Project. (2013). Available: www.pewinternet.org/

Polimeni, J. (2006). Transdisciplinary research: Moving forward. *International Journal of Transdisciplinary Research, 1*(1), 1–3, as cited in Damico, J., & Baildon, M. (2011). Content literacy for the 21st-century: Excavation, elevation, and relational cosmopolitanism in the classroom. *Journal of Adolescent & Adult Literacy, 55*(3), 232–243.

Postman, N. (1996). *The end of education: Redefining the value of school.* New York, NY: Alfred Knopf.

Richardson, W. (2010). *Blogs, wikis, podcasts, and other powerful Web tools for classrooms* (3rd ed.). Thousand Oaks, CA: Corwin.

Stephens, L. C., & Ballast, K. H. (2011). *Using technology to improve adolescent writing: Digital make-overs for writing lessons.* Boston, MA: Pearson.

Strong, W. (2006). *Write for insight: Empowering content area learning, grades 6–12.* Boston, MA: Allyn and Bacon.

Tallman, J. I., & Joyce, M. Z. (2006). *Making the writing and research connection with the I-search process* (2nd ed.). New York, NY: Neal-Schuman.

Teng, A. (2012, May). Writing teachers should comment on Facebook walls. *Voices from the Middle, 19*(4), 34–38.

Tompkins, G. E. (2013). *50 literacy strategies: Step-by-Step* (4th ed.). Boston, MA: Pearson.

Wheeler-Toppen, J. (2006). Helping students write about science without plagiarizing. *Science Scope, 29*(7), 47–49.

Wiggins, G., & McTighe, J. (1998). *Understanding by design.* Alexandria, VA: Association for Supervision and Curriculum Development.